PRAISE FOR
KENNETH C. ULMER

Bishop Kenneth Ulmer reveals from Scripture just how completely and fantastically our great God and Savior loves and cares for us, illuminating facets of His being that many believers have no doubt never considered.

Dr. Bill Bright
Founder of Campus Crusade for Christ

Dr. Ulmer is one of the most strategic Christian leaders in the nation. His impact in helping people understand God's principles for life is enriching while remaining biblical. It is hard to overstate the impact Dr. Ulmer makes on tens of thousands of Christians every week.

Dr. Mark Brewer
Senior Pastor, Bel Air Presbyterian Church, Los Angeles, California

Ken Ulmer is one of America's new voices, rising with a penetrating call to pragmatic spiritual dynamics. As a Christian leader, he stands tall; as a servant to society, he stands out; as a friend, he stands trustworthy; as a man of God, he stands close—in touch with our Father, that he might be in touch with Him whose touch can change the world. Knowing Dr. Ulmer as I do, I attest to this: the man is real to the core! The truths with which he inspires multitudes becomes real and livable because he is relating what he's learned and lived and proven.

Jack W. Hayford
President, Foursquare Churches International
Chancellor, The King's College and Seminary
Founding Pastor, The Church On The Way

Dr. Ken Ulmer does what he does best. He slices through the confusion, misunderstanding and misinformation and then clearly and accurately explains the Scripture.

Robert Morris
Bestselling Author, *The Blessed Life*

KNOWING GOD'S VOICE

KNOWING GOD'S VOICE

*Learn How to Hear God Above the Chaos of Life
and Respond Passionately in Faith*

KENNETH C.
ULMER

Regal

From Gospel Light
Ventura, California, U.S.A.

Published by Regal
From Gospel Light
Ventura, California, U.S.A.
www.regalbooks.com
Printed in the U.S.A.

Library of Congress Cataloging-in-Publication Data
Ulmer, Kenneth C.
Knowing God's voice / Kenneth C. Ulmer.
p. cm.
ISBN 978-0-8307-5890-6 (trade paper)
1. Listening—Religious aspects—Christianity. 2. Spirituality. I. Title.
BV4647.L56U46 2011
248.4—dc22
2011013122

Rights for publishing this book outside the U.S.A. or in non-English languages are
administered by Gospel Light Worldwide, an international not-for-profit ministry.
For additional information, please visit www.glww.org, email info@glww.org, or write
to Gospel Light Worldwide, 1957 Eastman Avenue, Ventura, CA 93003, U.S.A.

To order copies of this book and other Regal products in bulk quantities,
please contact us at 1-800-446-7735.

To my wife, Togetta.
You are the apple of my eye, the beat of my heart,
the wind beneath my wings.

Contents

Contents

Foreword

When I met Dr. Ulmer, I was immediately impressed with the obvious strength and nobility of his influence and leadership. He has discovered the fountainhead of all the greatest achievements that men and women have accomplished in the Kingdom, which is hearing and obeying the voice of God. Throughout biblical and Church history, it's almost impossible to find any great servant of Christ acting independently of God's guidance and achieving anything but disaster. As you read through the accounts of Moses, David, the prophets, Jesus, Peter, Paul, Martin Luther, John Wesley, Billy Graham, and so on, you will see that all had moments of encounter when God spoke to them and they obeyed.

In our fast-paced world, we desperately need to hear this message, urging us to stop, be quiet and listen so that we can do what we're meant to do, thus accessing all the strength, resources and divine circumstances made available to those who do the will of God. We are so in need of discovering the counsel of God instead of running to every other type of counselor available in our world today. The one thing David desired of God was that he would be able all the days of his life to enquire in the Temple and thus gain the guiding voice of God for his life. He knew this was the secret to living the blessed life. Dr. Ulmer's teaching on this, born from his own experience of hearing, doing and being blessed, will assist you to walk with Christ into your best life.

Dr. Phil Pringle
Senior Pastor, C3 Church, Oxford Falls, Australia
Founder, C3 Global (www.myC3church.net)

Such a Time as This

With increasing ferocity during the past decade or so, the world has been going through an unusually intense period of transition, including political upheaval, wars and rumors of war, and a stunning transference of wealth from the lower and middle classes to the upper economic echelons. These have been times of unparalleled poverty, increasing disease and wickedness in high places. Yet, the Lord has called us to the Kingdom "for such a time as this" (Esther 4:14). This is *our* time—a time when vast opportunities have opened up to expand the Kingdom of light in this world of darkness. All we need to do is *to know and to heed God's voice.*

We live in a culture that is more diversified, more cynical, more humanistic than at any time in history. Theological-religious and ethnic-racial pluralism has, in many parts of the world, disintegrated into devastating walls of division. Tension between the great monotheistic religions of Judaism, Christianity and Islam is poised like a sword over the necks of future victims of a coming storm. However, in these perilous times of spiritual sectarianism, sociological despair and ethical disparity, God continues to call to the church, saying, "Go therefore and make disciples of all the nations" (Matt. 28:19). Come out from the comfort of the padded pews and stained glass windows, and come into an atmosphere of obedience to God's Word as the return of the Lord draws near. In fact, God's marching orders to the church can be summarized in three commissions: (1) the Great Commission, (2) the Greater Commission, and (3) the Greatest Commission.

The Great Commission

We must never forget the mandate of the great commission, stated by Jesus in Mark 16:15, that we are to *"go into all the world"* (emphasis added). It is a call to decry the status quo and *do*. It speaks of the church as more than a bit player in a chaotic moment in time, or a mere "movement" that comes and goes. Indeed, the Lord is calling us to *be the move* of God, to be a dynamic organism, moving by His empowerment as head of the Church, and to go into all the world as witnesses for Christ's Kingdom.

In John 17:4, Jesus prayed, "[Father], I have glorified You." This verse gives the most succinct definition of what it means to glorify God than any other passage in Scripture. Jesus is saying that He has glorified God because He *completed the work God gave Him to do*. Therein lies Jesus' definition of "glorify": to *do* the work of the Lord. There is a sense in which we only glorify God if we do the work He gives us to do. Eugene Peterson captured the revelation of this verse in *THE MESSAGE* when he cited Jesus as saying, "I glorified you on earth by completing down to the last detail what you assigned me to do." That's what it boils down to. The church has for so long emphasized the "thou shalt not" of the Word, and has neglected the positive exhortations to "do." We only glorify the Lord to the degree that we *do* our assignment. Jesus glorified the Father by what He *did*. We glorify God by *doing* our assignment. If we don't *do* what He calls us to do, it doesn't matter how well we are performing our current task. And if we don't learn to *hear* from Him what He would have us *do*, then we are doomed.

What has God called you to do that you have not yet done? What are you neglecting while concentrating on other things? Maybe it's following through on that idea that has been brewing in your mind for so long. Maybe it's going back to school. Maybe it's handling your money differently. Maybe reading this book will reignite that creative spark in you to write your own book. What has He given you that you are not doing because you are putting your energies into something He called *someone else* to do? If you are still drawing breath, you still have work to do. *Go forth and* do *it!* We are not called to open the window of spiritual pomp and wave to the pilgrims admiring our ecclesiastical laurels. We are called, assigned and commissioned to "go" into all the world with the love, compassion and power of the Gospel, and to make disciples of the Lord Jesus Christ. That is our mandate. That should be our motive. *Go* should be our priority.

The Greater Commission

Jesus added an important condition to "go." As He met with His disciples for the last time before He returned to the Father, He told them, "Wait." For what? For the coming empowerment of the Holy Spirit (see Acts 1:4-5). This is the Greater Commission.

Jesus said, "Go." Yet, He knew He was calling these ordinary men to the extraordinary task of changing the world by making them disciples of Himself. He acknowledged their limitations by telling them that they were not quite ready to go. He told them to wait, and He would add something extra to their lives: the promise He told them about, His Holy Spirit. When God adds His extra to your ordinary, you have the power to do the extraordinary.

To go forth in the power of the Holy Spirit is the second commission the Lord presents to the church today. However, if we go forth in our own power, academic achievements, political connections and personal determination, then the moral, ethical and spiritual failures the world has watched the church struggle with for two thousand years will only continue.

The Holy Spirit gives us a practical power that enables us to live a God-honoring life before a sin-filled world. Even with the church's current emphasis on praise and worship, it is not the pseudo-entertainment atmosphere of upbeat music and quasi-spiritual gyrations that change lives. Lives are affected by hearing the Word of God given by the Spirit, by doing the will of God revealed by the Spirit and by walking the way of God guided by the Spirit.

The Greatest Commission

Finally, Jesus gave the Greatest Commission. In Acts 1:8, He said, "You shall receive power when the Holy Spirit has come upon you; and you shall be witnesses to Me in Jerusalem, and in all Judea and Samaria, and to the end of the earth." Did you catch that tiny word in that verse? He said that above all we shall *be* witnesses. There it is, the greatest commission: *be.*

The tension that the church faces today as we consider what we are to "be" in the world is the unquantifiable distance between being both attractive *and* authentic. In an attempt to be "attractive," we too often sacrifice authenticity, therefore representing nothing different to a world craving something better. To the other extreme, some of us have become so unrelentingly "authentic" that we drive away a dark and dying world. Yet, God wants more than that people leave church each Sunday "feeling better"; His desire is that we leave *being* better.

We are called to address the issue of poverty and therefore must minister to the poor. So, do we?

We must respond to the millions who are dying in the worldwide pandemic of AIDS/HIV. But do we?

The church (especially in America) must address the economic disenfranchisement of the masses by using our resources to create jobs and economically empower communities on a level that monopolizes our combined influence greater than individuals alone can achieve. Yet, are we?

As we continue to wrestle with anti-Americanism worldwide and anti-Islam sentiment here in America, we are called to love our enemies, confess our sins and ask for forgiveness. So, will we?

Such ministry, such aid, such economic empowerment, such change of heart and actions, must be done in the context of a message that is both authentic *and* attractive, for a great storm is descending upon the globe. More than 40 times in the Bible, the phrase "hear My voice," "heed My voice," "obey My voice" or some direct variation of the phrase appears. God's voice is His command. God's voice calls us to *be*, to *go*, and *do* during the most exciting time in history. He calls us to go into all the world with the message of the Kingdom of our Lord. That is the Great Commission. We are called to wait for the power of the Holy Spirit and then to go in the power of the Holy Spirit of the Living God. That is the Greater Commission. We are called to change the world by penetrating it in the power of the Holy Spirit who dwells in us, and by His presence to *be* His witnesses. That is the Greatest Commission.

The choice is ours: face the storm by seeking, learning and heeding the voice of God through the power of His Holy Spirit, and effect positive change in a world on the brink, or ignore His voice and perish.

More things are wrought by prayer than this world dreams of.
Wherefore, let thy voice rise like a fountain for me night and day.
ALFRED, LORD TENNYSON, *IDYLLS OF THE KING*

KNOWING
GOD'S
VOICE

1

The Lord Told Me!

Very early one morning many years ago, a woman called on the phone and announced, "The Lord told me that you are supposed to be my husband."

"Well," I responded hesitantly, unsure if it was a crank call or a strange dream, "what did He tell you I'm supposed to do with the wife I'm in bed with right now?"

There was a pause on the line and the woman said, "Well... um... God didn't tell me nothin' about that, Pastor. That's between you and her. I'm just telling you what He told me."

"Okay, then," I said, "as soon as He tells me, I'll get right back to you." And I hung up and went back to sleep.

Because of such strange "the Lord told me" stories, revelation from God is not a topic that people talk very much about. Yet, I'm sure that everyone at some time in their life has clearly sensed the Lord speaking to them. But it is the possibility of abuse and manipulation that can occur around the use of the phrase "the Lord told me" that causes many people to roll their eyes when the subject comes up. However, the truth is that if you have acknowledged and received Jesus Christ as your Lord and Savior, then you have actually heard God speak to you at least one time in your life.

There are probably countless times in your life when you have spoken to God. We've all asked God the "big" questions, such as:

Is this the person I should marry?
Should I accept this job offer or continue searching?
When will I recover from the economic meltdown?
What do You want me to do with my life, Lord?

Each of us has sought answers to these types of inquiries, hoping to hear God point the way for us. The good news is that God addresses every one of our inquiries, and He does respond to prayer. But the question most of us face in this modern, noisy world where God's voice seems to be increasingly drowned out is this: *How can I know for* certain *whether or not it's God I am hearing?*

In a world filled with endless distractions, conflicting input and occasionally even clashing theological viewpoints, is there actually a foolproof way to discern God's voice in the din? The short answer is *absolutely*. However, before we can learn and discern His voice, we must develop a two-way relationship with Him. And in order to do that, we first must learn *how* to hear God's voice.

If we don't hear God's voice in our spirit, then we can never be blessed with salvation, because, as Romans 10:17 points out, it is the Word of God that prompts us to consider faith in Him. This means that we have to read the Word or hear the message of the love and salvation that come through Jesus Christ preached before we can internally process its meaning and then profess a salvation faith. Thus, we must learn to discern God's unique voice when He speaks to our spirit—and that ability comes only from *relationship* with Him.

The first step in developing any relationship is simply to *listen*. Jesus often spoke to groups of thousands of people. There is no indication in Scripture that He ever used a megaphone or that He shouted to make sure the audience heard Him. Yet, there must have been hundreds of people at the far edges of those crowds who, listen as they might, had to strain to hear what He was saying. There are no verses in the Bible where Jesus asked the crowds, "Can you hear Me now?" It was, apparently, the responsibility of the listeners themselves to be in a position where they could hear His voice. If the crowds couldn't hear Him from where they were, then they had to get to a place where they could hear Him more clearly.

Since Jesus is no longer physically walking the earth and we can't go to a theater or auditorium or church or temple to hear Him speak in person, it is even more critical that we get ourselves in a position where we can hear what He has to say to us. But we live in noisy times, where it seems everyone has something to say, whether on the radio, television, telephone, Internet, billboards, bulletin boards, blogs, texts, instant messages, magazines, e-zines, newspapers, books, movies, and on and on and on—and they all want to be heard. So, is it possible to even *hear* God's voice over such a competing din of voices? It is. But it requires a relationship—and that requires a desire to pursue one, and an effort to build one.

Relationship

I believe that we all want to know how to hear God. When we learn to hear His voice, "He will teach us His ways, and we shall walk in His paths" (Isa. 2:3; Mic. 4:2). In fact, as John 10:3-4 indicates, the best way to follow the Lord is to learn His voice, because *He calls us by name*. Therefore, if we want to be able to respond and follow Him, we need to know His voice. And to learn His voice begins with having true *relationship* with Him.

Everything that I am going to write from this point forward in these pages is going to be with the assumption that you have (or with the appeal that you develop) a relationship with Jesus Christ. It is crucial for us to understand that each one of us Christians has heard God speak to us at some point in our life and that we have responded to His voice. Nonbelievers too have heard the voice of the God of the Bible speak to them. In fact, the Bible says that Samuel, one of the greatest prophets of biblical history, began both his relationship with God and his lengthy and powerful ministry as a young boy who did not yet know the Lord and before he had ever heard the voice of God (see 1 Sam. 3:7-9). Even still, once he heard God's voice, he had to be taught how to respond.

In this book, I am going to address the challenges of hearing the wisest guidance in a world of chaotic cacophony. We will examine what the Bible has to say about our individual role and responsibility in listening for God's voice. Then we will discover how we can get to the place in our lives where we know without a doubt when God's voice calls to us.

It is my desire that by the time you finish reading this book, the Spirit of the Lord will have created for you an atmosphere where you are comfortable saying, just as Samuel, the mighty prophet and leader of the Israelite nation, learned to say, "Speak, [Lord], for Your servant hears" (1 Sam. 3:10).

2

Can You Hear Me Now?

The question "Can you hear me now?" was once the catchphrase of a popular cell phone company's television advertising campaign that depicted a man talking into his mobile phone while trying to get into the right position so that the person on the other end could hear him. Over and over as he moved from one place to another, the man repeated, "Can you hear me now? . . . Can you hear me *now*?" The implication was that he was trying to get in a good position to be heard. The hook of the ad was that with this particular cellular telephone company, the communication process would continue unimpeded and that your voice could be heard from any position, no matter where you were located in the entire world.

Dr. Claudette Copeland, of San Antonio, Texas, is one of the most dynamic preachers I know. She once preached a powerful message at our church where she explained God's persistent desire to speak to us through the cacophony of challenging voices and competitive noises that vie for our attention every day. In a parody of this cell phone ad campaign slogan, she echoed God's loving determination to be heard by voicing His own repetitive question, "Can you hear Me now?"

That cell phone company's ad campaign could have come straight out of the Bible.

The Lord called Samuel. And he answered, "Here I am!"
So he ran to Eli and said, "Here I am, for you called me."

And he said, "I did not call; lie down again." And he went
and lay down. Then the LORD called yet again, "Samuel!"
So Samuel arose and went to Eli, and said, "Here I am,
for you called me." He answered, "I did not call, my son;
lie down again." (Now Samuel did not yet know the
LORD, nor was the word of the LORD yet revealed to him.)
And the LORD called Samuel again the third time. So he
arose and went to Eli, and said, "Here I am, for you did
call me." Then Eli perceived that the LORD had called the
boy. Therefore Eli said to Samuel, "Go, lie down; and it
shall be, if He calls you, that you must say, 'Speak, LORD,
for Your servant hears.'" So Samuel went and lay down
in his place. Now the LORD came and stood and called as
at other times, "Samuel! Samuel!" And Samuel answered, "Speak, for Your servant hears" (1 Sam. 3:4-10).

At the time the story in this passage took place, Samuel was
a young child, living in the quarters of the prophets, near the
temple. Before he was conceived, Samuel's mother Hannah (who
was barren) had made a deal with God. She told the Lord, "If
You . . . will give Your maidservant a male child, then I will give
him to the LORD all the days of his life" (1 Sam. 1:11). So, after
Samuel was born, Hannah took him to the temple where he entered the tutelage of Eli the priest, an elderly prophet and man
of wisdom who had been walking with the Lord for a long time.
Eli ministered to Samuel by teaching him how to hear and how
to respond to the voice of God.

Learning to Hear

Why is hearing God so important? Simply because the very core
of our relationship with God is that we walk by faith and not by
sight (see 2 Cor. 5:7). Anything we do in the context of our re-

lationship with God that is not of faith is sin, for we would be trusting in something other than in God. We must develop, nurture and guard our ability to hear.

One of the musicians in our church is Grammy Award-winning producer Warryn Campbell. Warryn makes his living by hearing. He is known throughout the music industry for his ability to hear the subtle nuances, harmonic possibilities and innovative potential of the precise blend of rhythm, lyrics and anointing in the myriad sounds of music. He once told me that he had to leave a hip-hop concert because the sound was so loud that he feared it would damage his hearing. One of the most precious disciplines we can learn is the ability to hear the voice of God. Just as an artist like Warryn Campbell makes his living by his ability to hear music, we make a life by learning to hear God's voice.

Many people think faith comes by doing. They try harder, they do more "good things," they mentally "pump up" their faith. But all that personal effort and activity, the Bible says, is not what produces faith. Romans 10:17 says that it is *hearing* that produces faith. Therefore, if we're not hearing God, then our faith is stunted or halted. And if our faith is not growing, then we are operating our life outside of faith—and everything we do places us outside of the will of God.

Eli said to young Samuel, "If He calls you . . . you must say, 'Speak, LORD, for Your servant hears'" (1 Sam. 3:9). You speak; I'm listening. You speak; I'm going to hear. Similarly, in the New Testament, Jesus repeats over and over the phrase, "He who has ears to hear, let him hear!" (Mark 4:9). This indicates that hearing God begins with three basic assumptions:

1. God has something to say to us.
2. We have the ability and capability to hear.
3. We deliberately *choose* to listen (or not to listen).

Why do we struggle so much with the issue of hearing God? Part of the reason is because many of us have become skilled at tuning others out. There have been times in my own life when I've put too much emphasis on praying *to* God and talking *to* God, and too little emphasis on hearing *from* God and listening *to* God. One stumbling block for many of us is that we were raised in, or are part of, a church environment or an ecclesiastical culture that gives the impression that prayer is a monologue where we say something to God and then we move on. In other words, we've been conditioned that our relationship with God is actually enhanced by our speaking and saying things *to* Him. Many of us even go through a one-sided communication ritual with an attitude that we love God so much that we want to let Him in on all our recent, late-breaking news: "This bulletin just in, from the life of Johnny Christian to God . . ." We give news flashes to God, oblivious of the fact that He knows what we need and what's on our mind before we even speak it to Him—actually, before we even *think* it.

What God really wants from us, though, is relationship with us where we speak *with* Him and listen *to* Him.

A Desire to Hear Him

Many people do not hear God simply because they have no desire to hear Him.

The *iconoclasts* tell God, "I've got this covered, Lord. I have it under control. If You find me in a fight with a bear, God, help the bear. I'm in good shape on this one. Don't need Your help, but thank You very much."

The *doubters* don't hear more from God because they struggle to discern the voice of God. They think things like, *Is this really God telling me this? Or is it me telling me? Or is it just my friend saying it?* Doubt and indecision freeze them.

The *leapers* get so spiritual that they boldly tell people, "The Lord told me!" Then, due to consequences that eliminate God as the source of their decision, they end up questioning God— never even realizing that it wasn't Him they were hearing in the first place. Leapers become disappointed in God when they realize it wasn't His voice they were hearing. I'm not talking about what color of shoes to wear to the party. I'm referring to a big decision they thought God was telling them to make. They ran off in one direction and then realized they were out there all by their lonesome selves when it turned out God wasn't involved in their choice at all.

Even though I have heard it more times than I care to admit, I am still a bit intrigued when I talk to a husband or wife who says, "The Lord told me to get a divorce." I usually reply, "Well, I thought you said the Lord told you *this* was the person you were supposed to marry." I think the most ironic reply I heard to that one was when a guy retorted, "Well, the Lord told me, 'You didn't ask Me when you married her in the first place, so don't ask Me for permission to divorce her. Whatever you do is okay with Me'," completely ignoring the marriage vows he took or the promise he made to his wife in front of witnesses.

It's so sad when we leap to the conclusion that the Lord has spoken, only to discover that He has said nothing, and the voice we thought we heard was the voice of our own passion or made-up mind.

The *non-selecteds* don't hear from God because they assume that He only chooses to speak to certain selected people who have a special connection to God. They think things like, *God probably speaks, but only to really spiritual people, not to me.* They believe that what it takes to hear from God is to pray, pray, pray, six or eight hours a day. The non-selected people tell the special connected, selected prayer warriors, "Hey, why don't you pray for me and tell me what God says."

The *fearful* are those persons who don't spend much time trying to hear God because they're afraid of what He might say. They've heard about coming before God in spirit and in truth. They do sort of want to go and bear their soul to Him, but they're terrified that if they really open up to God, He might say something like, "Whoa-whoa-*whoa* there! What's that right over *there* in your life? What are you going to do about *that* sin there?"

I often chuckle when I read the story of Jesus' encounter with the woman at the well. They are involved in a conversation that begins with Him asking her for a drink of water. Noticing her hesitancy (due to the tradition of those times, which discouraged interaction between Jews and Samaritans), Jesus tells her He is the source of water that will eternally quench her thirst. It is interesting, and kind of funny, that just as soon as she asks Him to give her some of that water, Jesus seems to switch the subject and tells her to go and get her husband. In a conversation that seems to be about water, Jesus redirects her attention to her personal life.

Some people are afraid of hearing from God for fear of what He will say to them. "W-well, Lord," they'd stammer if God confronted them, "that . . . *that's* not really what I wanted to talk to You abou—"

"—*No, no, no*—I want to talk about *that* stuff there that you're involved in!"

The fearful have sweaty flashbacks of that woman at the well who was trying her best to be spiritual when all of a sudden, Jesus asked her about her husband (because any thing or person or habit or attitude that we choose to stick with that takes us outside the will of God is our "husband").

The list goes on and on. People have endless excuses for not wanting to hear God. Growing in our relationship with God begins with a *desire* to hear Him and to hear *from* Him. If we are going to have a true relationship with Him, it must be one where we want to hear Him and where we strive to learn to listen to Him.

Revelation

Another big reason why many people don't hear God is because they go to Him with a laundry list. Their preset agenda is to address certain items, put in a request and then adjourn the meeting and get on with their life, preferably as quickly as possible. They "pray" things like:

Lord, should I do this or that?

Lord, should I go here or there?

Lord, can I have this or can I have that?

Lord, should I marry this one or that one?

They want to be told, "Do this. Take that. Don't go there." They don't want revelation from God; they only want information. But information only changes our thoughts (the way we *think* about an issue). The more information we have about something, the more we might think differently about it, but it is not information alone that changes our *behavior* about the issue. Only *belief* about something can change our behavior about that something. And there is only one thing that can alter, create or affect belief, and that is *revelation*.

Revelation alone is what alters one's belief. Once a person's belief has been altered by revelation, then that person's behavior will change. God is far more concerned about your behavior, but you will never adjust your behavior until you *believe differently* (through new revelation) about the issue in question. Just think back to when you didn't believe in God. There may have been absolutely no argument on earth that could have changed your mind about His existence. And then a revelation, through a seed planted by another person or through an experience you had or a thought process you went through, congeals within you. You do a one-eighty and you now believe in Jesus as the one and only Son of God. That complete change of heart that altered your belief came from *revelation*.

Concerning the things of God, then, revelation comes from the Holy Spirit, as the following Scriptures state:

Simon Peter answered, "You are the Christ, the Son of the living God." Jesus replied, "Blessed are you, Simon son of Jonah, for this was not revealed to you by man, but by my Father in heaven" (Matt. 16:16-17, *NIV*).

But as it is written: "Eye has not seen, nor ear heard, nor have entered into the heart of man the things which God has prepared for those who love Him." But God has revealed them to us through His Spirit (1 Cor. 2:9-10).

You will be able to understand my insight into the mystery of Christ, which was not made known to men in other generations as it has now been revealed by the Spirit (Eph. 3:4-5, *NIV*).

This paradigm of revelation-changing belief and belief-changing behavior could be charted like this:

BELIEF = BEHAVIOR
Enter: REVELATION
REVELATION *CHANGES* BELIEF
New BELIEF = *New* BEHAVIOR

Contrary to much common opinion, however, revelation does not always result in transformation. The journey of belief that impacts behavior is a process that is neither automatic nor simplistic.

Never was there, perhaps, more hollowness of heart than at present, and here in the United States. Genuine belief seems to have left us.

WALT WHITMAN, DEMOCRATIC VISTAS (1871)

Two Fundamentals Guide Your Life

Your relationship with God is based on two fundamental beliefs and ideas that determine how you live your life: (1) what you believe about God, and (2) what you believe about yourself. Let's examine each.

What You Believe About God

If you believe that God is truly your provider (I'm not talking about just singing a cute song about it, but truly knowing to a *certainty* that God provides), then that mindset determines how you will handle challenges that pop up throughout your life. For example, if you earn your living in commission sales, or if you're an artist who lives "gig to gig," or if you rely on residual income, when the checks are still arriving, then praise the Lord. But there may be times when your commission checks dry up; residual payments stop; and unemployment checks no longer arrive. That's when you've got to examine your mindset about what you really believe about God, because your rock-solid belief that "God shall supply all your need according to His riches" (Phil. 4:19) is what will help you make it through the lean times on your way to your next blessing from God (and will help you to *know* that your next blessing *is* out there somewhere).

Paul makes this statement with confidence because, as he said in Philippians 4:11, he has learned to be content no matter what the circumstances. The word that he uses for "learned" (the Greek word *manthano*) conveys the idea of getting acquainted with something, to come to know something, through a process of instruction and learning.[1] Paul has come to know something about God through a process in which God taught him. Paul doesn't just say, "God shall supply all your need" in a speculative vacuum of optimism. He says that the Lord has taught him, that he has learned something about God that shaped what he believes about God; and in verse 19, he says with the confidence of experiential faith, "My God shall supply all your need."

What you believe about God, based on what you have experientially learned about God through His revelation of His true character, will determine how you live your life. Our belief in God guides and affects our outlook, actions and reactions about the challenges and the blessings in our lives. For example, some people may not understand how you can go through all of the difficulties you've experienced and still come up with praise on your lips and joy in your heart. That is opposite to the thinking and reactions of the world. The playbook of the world is that when times are tough, you need to complain, whine, blame, threaten and worry. When the world sees you react with steadfast faith and calm trust in God, they simply cannot understand where you are coming from because they think that what you've been through should have caused you to lose your mind and flip out a long time ago. However, you know what God has promised, and therefore you believe that He will never leave you nor forsake you. You have learned to keep it together when voices of fear, worry, doom and gloom are pressing you to panic.

What we believe about God will shape how we live and how we approach the storms that come against us. Learning to hear the calm voice of God during the chaos helps nail down in our heart the basic truth, mind and spirit that *God will provide*. If we don't learn to distinguish God's voice from other voices, then we'd better get ready for some constantly churning emotions.

What You Believe About Yourself

The second fundamental belief guiding your relationship with God is what you believe about who you are as an individual. If you see yourself as God sees you, then you will recognize that there are boundaries in your life that will either affirm who you are in God (as you live within His boundaries) or will challenge your assertion of being a God-loving Christian (when you live outside of His boundaries). People who are confident about who they are in God will draw boundaries in their lives and will live within them.

There must be boundaries because within the circle of the will of God for our lives, there are things we must not tolerate, for to allow them into the circle of our existence would deny who we are as God's creation. We will refuse to live with some things because of who we are in God. We will not put up with certain behavior from others toward us or in our presence because of who we are as Christ's representatives here on earth.

In the book of Ephesians, Paul writes to the believers about their relationship with Christ. He says they were chosen before the foundation of the world and are predestined to live a life according to the will of God (see Eph. 1:4-5). The word Paul uses for "predestine" is the word *proorízœ*, which means "to set a boundary beforehand."[2] It is the idea of marking out limits before you get there; to establish in advance where the lines are. The blessings of God on our lives are within these boundaries. Our goal should be to live within the limits and boundaries that God sets for our lives. This is sometimes a challenging truth when we hear voices in our culture that suggest that there are no boundaries. Your dreams, goals and aspirations are to ultimately be fleshed out and attained within the boundaries of God's predetermined will for your life. That may sound restrictive (and maybe even frustrating), but I want to recommend the pattern and testimony of a rather obscure character in Scripture named Jabez.

Jabez is known primarily for being a man who got a prayer through to God: Jabez prayed a prayer and the Lord gave him what he asked for. His prayer was interesting. He simply asked God to enlarge his territory. There are various translations of his prayer in 1 Chronicles 4:10:

"Enlarge my border" (*NASB*)
"Make wider the limits of my land" (*BBE*)
"Give me a lot of land" (*CEV*)
"Extend my border" (*CSB*)
"Expand my territory" (*NET*)

The idea of the phrase is to expand or extend the boundaries or the limits of his territory. Jabez didn't ask the Lord to remove his boundaries, but to extend or expand or enlarge them. His goal was to live within the boundaries that the Lord set, but his prayer was that God would broaden those boundaries. It is an example both of submission to the Lord's will and of expression of faith in the God who sets boundaries in our lives.

As Christians, we represent the kingdom of God. Therefore, it is crucial that we live our lives based on our understanding and belief of who we are—and *whose* we are—in the circle of God's will. It is not that we feel we are better or more important than anyone else; it's that we are who we are as men and women of God. When David speaks of the person who lives life in honor and reverence to God (see Ps. 25:12-13), he says that person "shall dwell in prosperity" (v. 13). However, *The Living Bible* has a different spin on the verse, translating it as, "shall live within God's circle of blessing." This version speaks again of the concept of boundaries set by the Lord, but this time the picture is of the boundary within a circle. As an act of my will, I choose to live within the boundaries and circle of God's will, for it is there, within God's will, that I enjoy the blessings of God and the manifestation of His will for my life (we will cover this from another angle in chapter 7). Richard Smallwood puts lyrics to this idea in his song "Jesus, You're the Center of My Joy," when he sings, "All that's good and perfect comes from You."

God's goal is always that our choices and our behavior be shaped by our beliefs, and that our beliefs be shaped by revelation, not merely by information (which the world is brimming over with from every conceivable source). The revelation is of who we are inside in spite of where we are in our lives, because His voice within us is both our guiding beacon and our foundational anchor.

Out of heaven He let you hear His voice, that He might instruct you.
DEUTERONOMY 4:36

It All Began with His Voice

When God talks, He doesn't simply speak any language in the world—it's much more than that. And He doesn't just talk some "heavenly language"—it's far deeper than that, too. As Elihu, son of Barachel the Buzite, said in Job 33:14, "God may speak in one way, or in another." He talks how He talks—which is any way He chooses.

In the beginning, when God created the heavens and the earth, He "said" (see Gen. 1:3). What language did God speak when He "said"? When He spoke in the beginning, He was not speaking to a particular language group; He was speaking to "nothingness." Genesis 1:2 says that "the earth was without form, and void." In other words, the world was *nothingness*. This means that when God spoke, He spoke *reality* into existence from out of the nothingness. Thus, whatever He spoke into being came into being as a brand-new reality. For example, when He spoke, "Let there be light"—*BAM!* There was light.

A good analogy would be baking. My son, Kendan, is a chef. (I can't even boil water!) To watch Kendan in the kitchen is like watching a master artisan at work. As I am writing this, he is preparing for a family dinner. I hear the Lord's voice even as I watch my son cook. He prides himself in baking and preparing dishes "from scratch." The more I think about cooking from scratch, the more I imagine I hear the voice of the Lord telling me to call Kendan!

If you have ever baked a cake, you know that the basic ingredients include butter, sugar, flour, eggs, vanilla extract and milk. To make that cake, two things have to happen. First, you have to bring together the various ingredients, and second, you have to bake the cake. But you have to start with *something*; you cannot make a cake with nothing. In his book *Think Differently, Live Differently*, Bob Hemp highlights this principle.[3] Bob would say that when God is going to make a cake, He simply says, "Cake," and He's done. God speaks something out of nothing. Whatever you and I create must begin with some basic ingredients. We can't look at the oven and speak, "Cake," and have a hot cake suddenly sitting on the rack. We have to have something in order to get something. God needs nothing to get something. In fact, He specializes in getting something out of nothing. He starts with nothing, speaks something and that which was not, suddenly is, as though it always was.

Everything God created was created under the authority of His *speak*, so to speak. Regardless of the conditions when He speaks, He's the God who speaks reality into being. He can also change the reality of what we see into something that we can't see yet. And it all begins with His voice, His speaking.[4]

There may be areas in your life where you are discouraged by the circumstances in which you find yourself. But your reality is based only on your perspective, the facts that you can see, perceive and understand with your finite and limited awareness of your situation and your future. However, God *never deals in facts*;

He only deals in truth. Past, present and future for Him are all truth; and His truth trumps our facts every time. He's got a trump card that can speak truth into the facts of your challenges and struggles and change them into something completely different.

Through His Word

There are several ways God speaks reality into existence from out of nothingness. One way is through His Word, as the apostle Paul explains:

> All Scripture is given by inspiration of God, and is profitable for doctrine, for reproof, for correction, for instruction in righteousness (2 Tim. 3:16).

The Greek word for "scripture" is *graphe*, from which we get our word "graphics." It means "a document, i.e. a holy Writ (or its contents or a statement in it)."[5] In the context of the passage above, it means the holy writings, the Scriptures, the Bible. In other words, God talks about speaking through Scriptures, His written Word.

It is important to keep in mind that whenever we deal with the word of God from the perspective of Scripture, we must take into mind the historical period about which we are speaking. For example, in 2 Timothy 3:16 when the apostle Paul said, "All scripture," the Scripture Paul was referring to were the writings of the Old Testament (commonly called the "Law and the Prophets"). He was saying that God has spoken through His divinely inspired writing (what we would call the written Bible). Thus, one of the ways God speaks to us is through the writings He inspired through the prophets of both the Old Testament and the New Testament.

For example, maybe you've had something like this happen at some point in your life: You're experiencing a challenging situation and you read a particular passage in the Bible and *boom*— that Word gives you sudden revelation that pertains exactly to what you are going through. You think, "Ah-ha! The Lord has spoken to me." This is because God speaks to us through His written Word. You read a passage in the Bible, and it's like God is speaking directly to you. In that moment of revelation, that is God's word to *you*, specifically addressing your present challenge. And yet, that particular word existed long before you were created. However, this also reveals a conundrum: We know that God speaks to us through His Word, but His Word was written down long before our present circumstances. How can this be? The answer is that His Word is more than just that which is written down. The passage below helps explain:

> After these things the *word* of the LORD came to Abram in a vision, saying, "Do not be afraid, Abram. I am your shield, your exceedingly great reward" (Gen. 15:1, emphasis added).

In the verse above, the *word* came to Abram. "The word" cannot be referring to the written Scripture because the written word did not exist at the time this incident took place. This by no means diminishes the value of the written word, but in fact supports the reality that the Word of God was His word before it was ever written down. This account displays that God was, in effect, *speaking* His word before He inspired some 40-plus men to write down what He had already spoken. Here's the revelation and the mystery: God didn't just want these men to take dictation. He wanted them to paint a 100 percent reliable and accurate picture of Him. He wanted to *come alive* through His words. He wanted to be, in the Greek, the *logos*—"the word in flesh." That way, when He spoke, there would be no mistaking who was speaking and what He was saying. The verse below puts this in the clearest, most succinct terminology possible:

> For the word of God is living and active. Sharper than any double-edged sword, it penetrates even to dividing soul and spirit, joints and marrow; it judges the thoughts and attitudes of the heart (Heb. 4:12, *NIV*).

There are actually three different facets of representation and application of the Word of God in our lives: the *logos* word, a *rhema* word, and an *oracle*. Let's take a look at each.

The *Logos* Word of God

The "word of the LORD" that came to Abram in Genesis 15:1 is the same word of God found in Hebrews 4:12: the *living and active* word. At the time the writer of Hebrews spoke the words of Hebrews 4:12, the Word of God (in its totality) had not yet all been written down, so how could it be that "the word of God is living and active"? Can you hear a heartbeat in your Bible? Is the book actually walking around? Of course not. Yet, the writer says the word of God *is living and active*. What does this mean? In the New Testament, the most common word for "the word of God" is the word *logos*. *Logos* does not just mean "the written word"; it means "the substance" of the word, its *essence*. *Logos*, then, would be the representation of the word *if it were to come to life*.

In John 1:1, the word "Word" is capitalized (in every version of the Bible). This indicates that it is not referring to the thoughts expressed by the word; rather, it is talking about the actual personal embodiment of the word. Before the word was written (before it was even spoken), the substance, the manifestation, the physical representation of the word existed. "In the beginning was the Word, and the Word was with God, and the Word was God" (John 1:1) means that the Word is more than writing or speaking. It is living and breathing; it is real, visceral, an actual living entity. It's not just the written word of God or only an idea expressed in writing; it is the actual thing that the ideas speak of: It is Christ Himself—Jesus is *the Word*.

More than an Image

The concept of Jesus being God's word in the flesh is important to grasp because understanding it is *power*. For example, a photograph of me is just a symbol of me. If your only understanding of me comes from a snapshot of me with gap-teeth, bifocals, and hair all messed up, you would wonder why my wife ever married me. But, while that photo might even depict me fairly closely, *I* am not what is printed on that paper. *I* am the *logos*—the real deal, only *represented* by the image on the paper.

In other words, if you base your relationship with me only on what you see in that picture of me, then you and I will always have an inferior relationship, because what you see and believe are based on a fraction of reality. The "me" in that photo is *not* the real *me* any more than that picture could animate and come to life, step out of that image and shake your hand. That's because we live in a finite dimension governed by certain laws of physics that God put into place for this realm called earth. But God Himself is not constrained by such earthly rules of physics—neither on earth or anywhere else in the universe— which means that He can (and does) identically resemble the words in your Bible, because He *is* the words in your Bible. By this I mean that He is the truth, the very essence of the Bible as revealed in the flesh under the name of "Jesus of Nazareth." He's the incarnate living Word.

That may sound like a "deep" concept, but it's plain and simple. The apostle John painted the best picture of the "*logos* word" Jesus: "The Word became flesh and dwelt among us" (John 1:14). You can trust the Word of God because it *is* God.

A Devilish Distortion

The devil does not want you to understand that the Word became flesh and dwelt among us. The enemy wants to distort the picture you have in your mind about who and what God is, and about whether or not you can trust His Word and His voice. If the devil can distort your image of God, then he will distort and hinder your entire relationship with God. But that can only happen if you base your relationship with God on a distorted image of who, in fact, He is. The devil wants you to be in confusion and doubt about whether God speaks to you, about whether it's even possible to hear God's voice, and about the identities of the various voices that come at you during the average day. But if you want to learn God's voice and hear God's voice and distinguish God's voice from all others, then simply read His Word. *The Living Bible* states it this way: "Know what his Word says and means" (2 Tim. 2:15).

God is well aware of the scheming nature of the devil. So, in order to give us a real and accurate presentation of Himself, the God who is Spirit (see John 4:24) became flesh (actually reaching inside Himself and bringing out His "real self" wrapped in flesh and blood) and then set Himself down in a little town called Bethlehem, eventually sent Himself to the cross, went into a grave, and on the third morning raised Himself up with all power in heaven and earth. Now we see Him as He truly is, through the men He inspired to write truthfully and accurately about Him (and through revelation that the Holy Spirit deposits into our spirit, which we will discuss in detail in chapter 5).

God so loved the world that He gave Himself so that the *logos* picture of Him (the "word in the flesh") could not be distorted and we would get the real thing. When you see Jesus, you see God. When you love Jesus, you love God. If you want to know how God loves, you look at Jesus. If you want to know how God handles people, you look at how Jesus handled them—because Jesus is not a representation; He is the actual real deal.

A *Rhema* Word

The next word is the *rhema* word. While seeing the physical representation of the Word in flesh and hearing His wisdom and guidance and commandments are clearly essential, they are not *personal*. It doesn't necessarily take on intimate relevance to one person or to a certain group of people. However, there is another facet of the word of God that does make His voice personal, and that is the *rhema* word.

God loves us so much that He wants to make sure that His communication, His word, His voice are directed to us on a *personal*, individual level. The apostle Paul taught this in Romans 10:8 when he said, "The word is near you, in your mouth and in your heart." The Greek for "word" in Romans 10:8 is *rhema*, which means "an individual, collective or specific utterance."[6] Think of the "Word that became flesh" as God with skin on Him (Jesus). We know that Jesus is alive and active and real, but He's even *more* than that. The Word (God) came not just as the *logos* (physical) essence of God, but also as the *rhema* word; that is, the deliverance of the word to a *particular person* in a *particular set of circumstances* at a *particular time*.

By comparison, the *logos* word and a *rhema* word can be stated like this:

The *logos* word (the written word) is the *physical essence* of the word of God. The *rhema* word (the spoken word) is the physical essence of the written word *made personal*.

A *rhema* word is never a general word to people in general; it's a *personalized* word to a specific person or group of people. For example, a *rhema* word is not just that God so loved the world; it is that God so loved *you*. It's when God speaks to *your* specific personal situation.

Romans 10:8 indicates that the *rhema* word is already here, it's in your mouth, which means that you should begin to speak what God has spoken to you—and *believe* it. The word is here, the revelation is here, the unveiling is here, so God says now you must speak it. It's in your mouth to speak, and it's in your heart, because with the heart you believe unto salvation.

An Oracle Word

The third word is an "oracle." The word "oracle" is *logion* in Greek, which is a diminutive form of the word *logos*. An oracle means "a little word," a brief, personal word specifically *about a word* that has already been given. The oracles of God are more refined *rhema* teachings; they're more like sentences or utterances as opposed to the totality of the *rhema*.

In the book of Hebrews, when the believers were confronted about their spiritual immaturity, the writer said to them that by now they should be so skilled in the Word that they should be teachers; but instead, they needed to go back and relearn again the first principles of the oracles of God (see Heb. 5:12). This is the idea of the basic rudiments, the fundamental sentences or foundational utterances of God. It would be like saying that although you should be writing books and teaching them by now, you are so far behind that you need to go back and learn the *ABCs*—the very fundamentals of the Word of God. Oracles, then, are prophetic revelations that God has already released that ought now be applied to *your* specific situation.

Here is a succinct comparison of a *rhema word* with an *oracle*:

The Romans 10:8 *rhema* word "the word is near you" is that *God loves you*. The *oracle* of the Romans 10:8 *rhema* word would be that God loves you *right where you are now, no matter what*.

The flow of the apostle word to the *rhema* word to an oracle would be this:

God speaks His apostle Word to mankind as ⌒ Jesus. Jesus speaks God's Word to each of us as ⌒ a *rhema* word. The specific message in the *rhema* Word is ⌒ an oracle word spoken to apply *specifically to you*.

An oracle is not a long revelation. It's not a sermon. It's not even a class or a teaching or a book. It's just a sentence or two. It's simply when God speaks to your spirit during those times when you're caught in the clutches of reality. A *rhema* word is personal; an oracle is more *intimate*. It's when God speaks to you at the time when you're feeling like you are out there all by yourself. It can be when God reminds you that He'll never leave you, as simple as, "You're coming through this" or "I'm still here with you" or "Remember, you made it through this just fine the last time it happened." It's a little word that packs an important punch. It's something that you need to hear from God at a specific time in your life. It's when "a little dab'll do ya," so to speak. Most of you are probably too young to have any idea what that phrase means, but it's a throwback to the theme of a Brylcream hairdressing product from the 1950s: you didn't need much of it to get a well-groomed coif—just a little dab'll do ya. (Okay, so I'm a little old school; but you get the point.)

An oracle can also be something like, "You better straighten up there, man." An example of this appears in the book of Acts after the disciple Stephen had been charged with blasphemy and dragged before the council of elders and scribes. In his response in Acts 6 to the charges leveled against him, Stephen recounted Jewish history to them, starting with Abraham, Isaac, Jacob, Joseph, all the way through Moses and Solomon, reminding them that their forefathers had repeatedly disobeyed God's commands. Then Stephen closed with countercharges against the Jewish leaders that *they* had killed Messiah Jesus.

Stephen's recounting of history to his accusers was a *rhema* word to them. His closing remarks to that *rhema* word were an oracle, directed specifically at the council leaders:

You stiff-necked and uncircumcised in heart and ears! You always resist the Holy Spirit; as your fathers did, so do you. Which of the prophets did your fathers not persecute? And they killed those who foretold the coming of the Just One, of whom you now have become the betrayers and murderers, who have received the law by the direction of angels and have not kept it (Acts 7:51-53).

When the council leaders heard these things, "they were cut to the heart, and they gnashed at him with their teeth" (Acts 7:54). "Cut to the heart" means that their consciences were pricked, and they became angry at Stephen for what he said about them. Their response should have been to give thanks to him for the reminder that they were off course, and to repent for what they were doing. Instead, they gnashed their teeth in anger at Stephen's countercharges, and then they murdered him—doing exactly what he had accused their fathers of having done.

They discounted the *rhema* word that should have taught them, and they ignored the oracle that could have saved them.

When You Need Him *Now*

Sometimes you don't need a whole sermon. Sometimes all you need is just a little word to get you through, to keep you on track. I've gotten emails and texts when I've been going through particularly challenging trials, little notes where someone has said, "God's word promises He won't let you down." In the midst of tough situations, we need those oracles. Sometimes you can't make it all the way until church on Sunday. If you only expect God to speak when you're at church, at best you'll only hear Him once every seven days. Our problem isn't always about Sundays; it's the trying things we go through Monday through Saturday as we're on our way to Sunday. We've got to have a little word to pull us through the week. We need something to hold us until we get back into church to hear the big Word. Right now, we need just a little word, a revelation, an oracle, a prophetic utterance. We need the Lord to speak to us *now*.

Smokie Norful, the extremely talented gospel singer from Chicago, soared on the airwaves with his faithful plea to the Lord in his smash hit EMI Gospel song "I Need You Now." There is a line in the hymnody of the African American tradition that says, "He may not come when you call Him, but He's always on time." In the frustration of my fleshly experience, I cry out to the Lord, "I need You now!" My "now" may not always be God's now, but His now is *always* on time.

Wait on Him to Speak

God wants to speak in this generation in this second decade of the new millennium. He wants to release a word into our reality. He specifically wants to change *our* reality, to personalize His word to us. He wants to release a little word that's just enough to keep moving forward in life with Him.

To know what God is wanting to say to us, to hear Him *now*, we need to ask God something like this: "Holy Spirit, what are You saying to me? Speak to my heart, Lord. Speak the words I need to hear to get me from here to there." And then wait for His answer.

The greatest discipline God wants to teach us is the discipline of waiting on Him to speak because the pattern of too many of us has been to give Him about a minute or so, and if He hasn't spoken by then, we take the thing in our own hands and do what we want to do anyway.

What area of your life do you need the Lord to speak to? Eli told Samuel to say, "Yes, Lord, I'm listening" (1 Sam. 3:9, *TLB*). Some of us need to learn to do something we have never done before: wait on God to speak. He may not speak until next week. He might not speak till tonight or until next month. But He *will* speak!

> *Speak to my heart, Holy Spirit*
> *Give me the words that will bring new life*
> *Words on the wings of the morning*
> *the dark night will fade away*
> *If you speak to my heart.*
> DONNIE MCCLURKIN, "SPEAK TO MY HEART"[7]

Notes
1. James Strong, *Strong's Dictionary* (Nashville, TN: Thomas Nelson, 1996), Greek #1329.
2. Spiros Zodhiates, ed., *The Complete Word Study Dictionary: New Testament* (AMG International, Inc., 1993).
3. Bob Hemp, *Think Differently, Live Differently* (Dallas, TX: Thinking Differently Press, 2010).

4. In fact, when God speaks it, His voice isn't even the start of the process of becoming something; rather, it reveals that the something is *already* what He said it is.

5. Strong, *Strong's Dictionary*, Greek #1124.

6. Ibid., *rhema*, Greek #4487; from Greek #4483: "an utterance (individual, collective or specific)."

7. Donnie McClurkin, "Speak to My Heart," © 1996 Word Entertainment.

3

Lord, Is that You?

Would you agree to do whatever someone asks you to do before they tell you what they want you to do? Most people probably would not, even if it was someone close to them doing the asking. A first response might be something like this: "Tell me what you want me to do, and then I'll decide if I'm going to do it." Others might say, "Well, let me think it over."

There is only one reason somebody would say "yes" to a question like that without first asking for specifics: *trust.* You would probably be more likely to do what someone asks of you without knowing what they're going to ask only if you have a *relationship* with them. In the context of that relationship, you have built up enough trust to say "yes" to a blind request. For Christians, the issue of trust raises an important question: "If you trust a friend or loved one so much that you would seriously consider doing whatever they might ask, do you trust God that much?" Can you say, "Yes, Lord, I'll do it," without asking what He is going to request of you? Many Christians have problems obeying God's word because they have learned neither how to hear Him nor how to recognize His unique voice.

However, before we can know God's voice, we must first *know* God. And, as we covered in the previous chapter, knowing God comes from having a relationship—and it is that relationship that builds trust. Once you have a relationship and you develop trust, when He asks something of you, you no longer need to respond with, "Lord, is that You speaking?" Since you already know it's Him, your response is, "Your will be done."

The key is to develop such a relationship of trust in God that His voice alone becomes our assurance, as the apostle John stated:

> And when he brings out his own sheep, he goes before them; and the sheep will follow him, for they know his voice. . . . My sheep hear My voice, and I know them, and they follow Me (John 10:4,27).

In the verses above, Jesus says that His sheep know His voice. This means that God has included in our relationship with Him the *ability* to recognize and to hear His voice. In other words, God is telling us that because we are His children, we should know His voice. However, just as a child must learn to recognize the voice of its parents from among other voices, you and I must *learn* to recognize the voice of God before we can know His voice.

As His sheep, God's people hear His voice and follow Him. This indicates that they are in such a relationship with God that they trust Him implicitly. They know His voice, they hear His voice, they obey His voice. (It's interesting to note that the apostle who recorded the words in the verses above was the apostle John—also known as "John the Beloved"—who had probably the closest relationship with Jesus.)

When Jesus was ministering, a large crowd of people always surrounded Him. From out of a crowd, He would choose, for example, 70 people to perform a special task (as in Luke 10). Beyond those 70, he had a chosen 12 known as the apostles. From out of the 12 apostles, Peter, James and John were considered Jesus' inner circle. Out of those three, it was generally thought that John had the closest relationship with Jesus. John was the apostle at the cross when Jesus was crucified. John was the one who sat next to Jesus at the Last Supper and leaned against Him as they ate. And it was John, the apostle who so deeply loved Jesus, who wrote the verses about the sheep knowing their master's voice and obeying him unquestioningly. Clearly, John had pursued and developed a close relationship with the Lord and had his ear tuned to God's voice.

Learning God's Voice

It all starts with learning God's voice. One of the reasons some Christians have a hard time hearing God's voice is because they have not learned to *recognize* His voice.

Learning different voices and how to distinguish them from others is one of the first things that human beings learn. Babies must learn the voices of their mother and father. There is nothing innate in an infant that automatically helps the child know his or her mother's voice from his or her father's voice, or those two voices from all other voices in the widening circle of the infant's relatives and family friends. The special time that parents spend with the child in the early weeks and months after he or she is born is often spent doing two things: looking in the baby's face and talking to the baby. Regardless of what is being said, the little child is familiarizing himself with, and becoming acclimated to, the voices of his or her parents.

There's something special about the voice of a parent due to the relationship between the child and the parent. If, for example, my baby granddaughter Aniya were to be lifted up in church one Sunday and everybody called out her name, she would probably turn in the direction of the voices, but she wouldn't respond much more than that. However, if her mother or father called to her, she would recognize the voice and she would display a noticeable response because she has learned to recognize those two particular voices. Likewise, a baby can be crying and nobody can soothe the baby, but when the mother comes and coos, "Don't cry," the baby usually begins to calm down.

My granddaughter really embarrassed me one Sunday in my office after church. She was having a crying spell—actually, it was more like a screaming spell. I went over to her, and in my grandfatherly voice I began to calmly talk to her. Many times I had seen her calm down when I took her in my arms and began to quietly talk into her ear. I assumed this would be the case this time, too. In fact, the room full of people had watched me—indeed, urged me—to go over to her, expecting me to calm the voice of this little person who had taken charge of the room with shrieks that indicated she wanted something.

In my usual grandfather swagger, I made my way over to Aniya, expecting her crying to gradually diminish. Not so! I tried my usual tender whisper into her little ear. Nothing. I tried holding her and gently rocking her in my arms. She continued wailing. In fact, it was as if she got more upset because I seemed to have the gall to try to quiet her down. What embarrassed me the most was the look on her little face that seemed to be saying, "Don't even try to calm me down, Grandpa!" In the midst of the laughs and snickering and frustration of the group of people (who had by now focused all of their attention on my screaming little grandbaby), her mother stepped to her and said, "Now, why are you crying?" And the crying instantly ceased. That's all it took; the child's shrieks were immediately silenced. The tantrum was curtailed. She had stopped her screaming at the mere sound of her mother's voice and was utterly calmed.

There is something about the calming voice of the Lord that speaks peace and comfort and serenity into our spirit. May you know His voice. May you know the peace that God speaks.

To Recognize a Voice

The process of learning to recognize one voice from another involves developing the ability to distinguish three aspects about voices: sound, style and substance. Let's look at each one.

Sound

Before children begin to learn different vocal sounds and speech patterns so they can distinguish their parents from other people, they must first learn to recognize the *sound* that each particular voice makes. As a child lays in its crib or bed, or as it is being fed or played with while the mother or father is speaking, the child is learning the particular sound of each parent's voice. The mother's voice may be higher in pitch than the father's voice. The father's voice might be deeper than the mother's voice. The child learns to recognize the *sound* of its parents' voices. The sound of the voice of the parent and the child's ability to recognize and heed it are significant dimensions of the relationship that is developing between the parent and the child.

> *An intimate love relationship with God*
> *is the key to knowing God's voice, to hearing*
> *when God speaks. You come to know His voice*
> *as you experience Him in a love relationship.*
> HENRY BLACKABY AND CLAUDE KING, *EXPERIENCING GOD*[1]

Style

The child is also learning the *style* of each parent's voice, the peculiarity of the tone, the pitch, the cadence, whether the person talks fast or slowly, halted or fluidly, muffled or clearly. For example, there's something in the manner in which a mother can coo, "Don't cry, honey. Don't cry, baby." There's something calming about a mother's voice. A baby can be crying and no-body can stop the baby from crying (as I found out with little Aniya!), but when the mother comes in and says, "Don't cry," the child recognizes not only the sound but also the style, and reacts. However, if someone else was holding that baby and say-ing, "Please don't cry. Come on, stop crying," the child would learn to distinguish the communication style difference be-tween one voice and another and react accordingly.

Thus, the baby learns to recognize not merely the voice alone, but the pattern of speech, the inflections and the atti-tude of the delivery. All of these different aspects make up the particular *style* of the parents' voices that the child is in the pro-cess of learning.

Substance

Finally, children learn to understand and recognize the *sub-stance* of the voice; that is, what the parent is saying. There is something soothing about the words of a parent because of the relationship between that child and the parent. Words like, "It's going to be okay. Don't cry, sweetie. It's all right," are soothing words in themselves that, when delivered with the style and sound of the mother, help the baby learn to connect with the mother. The infant is in the process of learning to recognize the particular substance of the voice of its parents from all other voices. Substance eventually leads to cementing familiar-ity, establishing trust and eliciting reactions.

Audible Infants

We hear so many competing voices in society today that, in the same way a child must learn to recognize the voices of its par-ents, you and I need to be able to learn to discern with certainty when we are hearing God's peculiar voice.

Have you ever been praying and heard a voice in your spirit and wondered, *Was that me thinking or was that God speaking?* We hear voices in our spirit all right. Some people just can't always discern spiritually to whom the voices belong. They are "audible infants." Part of the learning process is to get to the point where we can say with certainty, "Now, *that's* God speaking" or "No, that's not God's voice."

There are three things that identify God when He speaks: (1) God speaks with authority; (2) God speaks principles that are truth; and (3) God speaks through circumstances. Let's examine each of them.

Authority

There's a particular sovereign power to God's voice when He speaks:

- With authority He commands (see Mark 1:27).
- His word was with authority (see Luke 4:32).
- With authority and power He gives orders (see Luke 4:36).

In Mark 4:39 when He commanded the storm, "Peace, be still," the winds and the waves immediately calmed down. Authority does not argue. Authority does not bargain. When God speaks, He speaks with authority. He spoke and the winds stopped and the waves calmed. "Peace, be still!" Jesus spoke with authority. He did not invite debate.

Principles

God has spoken (and still speaks) through His Word. Dr. Tony Evans says, "God has spoken and He did not stutter."[2] In fact, He speaks most often through principles in His Word. What this means is that God will never speak a word that contradicts any of the principles contained in the Bible. For example, you cannot turn to a verse of Scripture and find out specifically whom you should marry. However, God will tell you that whoever your marriage candidates are, they should be holy and godly, and that you are not to be unequally yoked together with an unbeliever (see Lev. 11:44-45; 2 Cor. 6:14).

Some people believe that if they're simply not happy in their marriage, God will cut them some slack, and they can leave the marriage and go find someone else. But any word we hear that contradicts God's Word cannot be from God. There is no wiggle room with the principles of the Lord. His principles do not waver. His principles do not argue. Jesus is the same yesterday, today and forever (see Heb. 13:8).

Circumstances

God also speaks through our circumstances. There is a saying that goes, "God opens doors and closes doors." That's true; He does speak through circumstances and opportunities. The book of Acts, for example, tells about when Paul tried to go this way, but the door was closed. Then he tried to go another way, and again the door was closed.

We can all handle a closed door here and there; it just helps to learn to distinguish *who* closed it. Everyone likes a door opening; we only need to learn to discern whose hand is on the knob.

Spirit, Will and Flesh

One of the ways God speaks to us is through thoughts, ideas and impressions that He speaks into our spirit. For instance, when you have an eye-opening impression or a new revelation about something important, that's one of the ways He speaks to you.

For some Christians, that type of word is fairly elementary and common. For other Christians, when God speaks into their spirit that way, they may take it as a deep and otherworldly experience. They may announce something like, "Thus sayeth the Lord unto me." Sometimes the Lord did say something to them, but He didn't say what they claim He said. If these Christians haven't taken the time to develop a relationship with God enough to know His voice, how can they be so sure it actually was His voice?

In addition to the three things that identify God's voice when He speaks, there are also three different voices that want to speak to a different aspect of our being. Yet, only one of these voices is the voice of God. Here are some basic guidelines for discerning exactly who is doing the talking:

1. God will always speak into our spirit.
2. The devil speaks to our flesh and to our will.
3. We speak to our flesh.

Take, for example, God speaking these words into someone's spirit: "I want you to go over there and go up those steps." Some people might get panicky and respond with something like, "What, Lord? You want me to go *all* the way up *all* of those long steps over there? But I don't know if I can make it all the way up those steps. If You just want me to go up some steps, how about letting me go up these shorter steps over here? I'd rather go up these than those."

At this point, because the devil knows that we will always wrestle with our flesh, the minute he sees us waver at the sound of God's voice, he will get in there and entice our flesh, speak to our will, and press and shove and cajole us to do something other than what God told us to do. That old devil will say something like, "God said for you to go over there and go up those steps. But the reason He's ordering you to do that is because there's something on this side over here that He doesn't want you to see—something you will like even more. If you come this way instead of going that way, then you will find everything you've been looking for, right up these steps on this side. Trust me."

Even Jesus was subjected to the devil's voice. In Matthew 4:8-9, when Jesus was being tempted in the wilderness, the devil took Him up to a high peak and showed Him all the kingdoms of the world. He said to Jesus, "All these things I will give You if You will fall down and worship me."

Listen, Learn and Experience

We know the voice of God by *listening* to it, *learning* it and *experiencing* it. Likewise, when we've learned the voice of the devil and have experienced how he speaks and sounds, then the next time he comes back at us with his enticements, we should have learned how to recognize his lines from the last time he went at us—and this time around, we should have a strategy to bind him and come against him. If you already experienced what happened the last time the enemy spoke and you listened and suffered the consequences, then you won't listen to his voice as he tries to pull his deceptions on you this time. You will have learned that when the devil speaks, "he speaks his native language, for he is a liar and the father of lies" (John 8:44, *NIV*).

The devil has been watching us since the day we were born. He learns about us by his experience with us and his observations of us. He and his minions know *everyone's* weaknesses. He studies each of us carefully, getting to know us *very* well during our lifetimes. He has a file with each of our names on it in his Rolodex so he can customize his enticements to each hearer. There are lures the devil uses for one person that he won't use on another because what he offers to one won't be attractive to the other. His voice of temptation won't necessarily come against you with what he says to me, because you are not tempted by what I am. There are things you will fall under the temptation of that I have overcome.

One of my first jobs out of college was in sales. I was taught that when I had pitched a product to a potential customer but they didn't buy, I was to make note of the attempted transaction in a "tickler file," which was a reminder that while I missed selling the customer that time, I should go back to them and try again at some future date. The devil has tickler files on each one of us. He knows that if his sales pitch doesn't work on us today, all he has to do is put us in his tickler file and come back at us another time. He's an experienced and persistent salesman.

God's Voice Lifts

The LORD will give strength to His people; the LORD will bless His people with peace. . . . I will extol You, O LORD, for You have lifted me up.
PSALM 29:11–30:1

So, what does God's voice sound like when He speaks? What is the style of His speech? What is His attitude, His spirit, His approach and the consistent thrust of His messages to us? God has many approaches. For example, as Isaiah 42:3 states, a bruised reed God will not break. This means that God will never come to you when you're down and then drain you of your remaining strength. Then there's 1 Corinthians 14:33, which says that God is not the author of confusion. In other words, God will never speak a word to you that brings disorder, but of peace. As we will study in chapter 4, if you begin at Psalm 29:3 and read through the psalm, you'll discover that He speaks peace in the midst of storms. He interjects Himself and speaks over the waters that are raging, the thunder that is rolling and the mighty waters that are churning. He says, "My peace I give you. I do not give to you as the world gives" (John 14:27, *NIV*).

The examples go on and on. Note, for example, the gentle, encouraging, nonjudgmental tone Jesus takes with the woman in the passage below:

> When Jesus had raised Himself up and saw no one but the woman, He said to her, "Woman, where are those accusers of yours? Has no one condemned you?" She said, "No one, Lord." And Jesus said to her, "Neither do I condemn you; go and sin no more" (John 8:10-11).

In this passage, the scribes and Pharisees had brought to Jesus a woman they had caught in the act of adultery. Jesus responded with compassion. The voice of guilt is not the voice of God. Every whisper, every shout, every reminder of guilt in your life is not from God, because when He speaks, He says, "Neither do I condemn you." Rather, He corrects us ("go and sin no more"). His correction comes without condemnation while pointing us in the right direction.

He speaks words of direction, correction and confirmation:

1. *Direction*: He puts us on the right road. "This is the way."
2. *Correction*: He tells us when we are off the road. "It's not that way; it's this way."
3. *Confirmation*: He affirms that we're on the right road. "Stay your course. It may get rough, but you're on the right road. Don't look to the left or to the right. Don't give up on what I've told you."

Here is one foolproof way to know that it is God speaking and not you: God is smarter than we are! He comes up with things we could never think up ourselves—we're not that wise or intelligent. He calls us to do things that challenge us, that encourage us to rise up. He puts targets in front of us. He sets goals before us. He gives us direction that we can't always come up with on our own. I don't know about you, but I'm not smart enough to think up many of the things I accomplish. I'm not clever enough to get these ideas all by myself, so it must be God. I've learned to say to Him, "Speak, Lord. Let it roll. I'm listening."

You may be doing things right now that you never imagined you could do. Every time anybody put it in your mind to do what seemed impossible, the enemy probably tried to convince you that you're too much this, you're not enough that, you came from the wrong side of town, you come from bad stock, you have no initials behind your name, you haven't been through enough testing or trials, or you've done too many wrong things in your life. But when God has something for you, even the devil in hell cannot stop you from getting it. And if you don't get it by trying over here, then just hold on—He's got it for you over there. Trust His voice—go and do what God told you to do!

There will always be the nay-saying folks, the haters, who will try to nullify or drown out the voice of God by telling people what they cannot do. Too many people come at us with the voice of discouragement, saying things like, "You bit off too much now, didn't you?!" *Bit off more than I can chew?* I don't have to chew it myself! God will send somebody to chew this bad boy up for me, and I'll move ahead and do exactly what He told me to do!

Don't ever let somebody tell you what you can or cannot do. Listen to the voice of God—He's smarter than you are. That's why I enjoy graduation time. I like to see single mothers out there being handed a college diploma when people said they couldn't make it, when they were wondering how they were going to pay the tuition bills and keep food on the table. All the while, God continued to provide and kept speaking into their ear, "You can do exceeding abundantly above all that you ask or think" (see Eph. 3:20).

When God's Voice Says "Jump!"

After God speaks, you must *act*. It is what He is saying to you *now* that you must act on, because He is the one who positioned the circumstances, spoke His word and released into your spirit the desire to do it. "Now," He says, "*do it*." That's where faith comes in. When you hear His voice, respond in faith.

When I was a little boy, Superman was my hero. I loved to play Superman. I would wrap a little bathroom towel around my neck as a cape, and I'd climb up the big staircase we had in our house. Don't mess with a little guy with a towel on, ready to fly down the stairs, I'm telling you! My daddy would stand at the bottom of those stairs, look in my eyes, and speak one word that was filled with power and encouragement and glory and energy: "JUMP!"

I'll never forget it. I had my little towel on. I was poised on the steps. I was ready to fly. I was breathing fast. It was a long way down. I heard Daddy's voice say, "Okay, now. Jump! Jump, man, c'mon—*jump!*"

When you jump off of stairs like Superman, you have to put your hands out in front of you and leap. My heart would beat faster and my eyes would get big as golf balls as I wondered if I was going to splat facedown onto the floor this time. "Don't let me fall, Daddy!" I'd cry out nervously. "Don't step back, Daddy! Don't you miss me! Don't you miss me, Daddy!" I knew his voice and I trusted him because I had jumped before. The routine was always the same: I'd jump and hang there in midair with my eyes glistening in wide-eyed terror while trying to disguise it to look like Superman-determination instead of fear. And every time, Daddy did the same thing: just about the time when it looked like I was going to hit the floor, Daddy would dip down, reach out, scoop his arms under me and catch me.

"Gotcha!" he would shout triumphantly, his eyes gleaming. My little face would be beaming with joy, relief and exhilaration. I was Superman! And my daddy was there to make sure of it.

The Lord is telling you today, "Get your cape. Put on your faith. And get ready to jump. Because you can trust My voice. I didn't let you fall last time. I'll catch you every time. Just trust me . . . and *jump!*"

Leap out in faith, and before you hit the ground, you'll see God's actions say, "Gotcha!"

Speak, LORD, for Your servant hears.
1 SAMUEL 3:9-10

Sometimes hanging in midair in life with a towel around your neck does seem a little crazy, I must tell you. But the principle is simple: *gotcha!* So I say, "Speak, Lord, for your servant will hear and obey."

Notes
1. Henry Blackaby and Claude King, *Experiencing God* (Nashville, TN: Broadman & Holman, 2004), p. 138.
2. Anthony T. Evans, Th.D., *How Christians Are Destroying America,* www.Tony Evans.org

4

You Can't Hear from There

As I mentioned briefly in the introduction, when I read scenarios in the gospels where Jesus is speaking, I'm often reminded that He had no microphone, no megaphone, no type of public address system at all whenever He spoke to the crowds of thousands who followed Him around. No amplification systems, no equalizers, no woofers, no bass or treble. Just His voice.

There must have been people in those crowds who had to strain to hear Him because they couldn't hear from where they were. We never read that He walked among the crowd as He was speaking or that He ever asked the people, "Can you hear me now, can you hear me?" It always seemed that hearing Him was the responsibility of the hearers. As the crowds became larger and His voice maybe became strained from having to speak more loudly, after a while it might have seemed as though hardly anybody could hear Jesus speak. He was, after all, in a human body, with its physical endurance limitations.

Sometimes when I preach in church on Sundays, I notice that some people have switched seats from the previous week and are sitting somewhere else. So now they're in a different position, listening to me from a new location. The environment is different on one side of the church than on the other. The angle is different. If you're sitting on one side, you have to turn one way. If you're sitting on the other side, you turn the other way. You hear more from one location than the other because your ability to hear is relative to your position.

There's a strange paradox about the idea of hearing God, an odd inconsistency that every one of us struggles with—often without even knowing we're struggling: on one hand, most of us (for the most part) probably truly desire to hear from God, but on the other hand, even in the face of our sincere desire to hear from Him, the reality is that most of us aren't really sure when He's speaking or if what we just heard in our spirit was from God. There are times when we truly want to hear from God, and we'll seek to hear Him, and we'll hear *something* . . . but we don't know if it was really God or not. You're not "unspiritual" if (or when) that occurs in your life. It's just that because of the finality and the limitations of our humanness, we must learn not just the unique sound of the voice of God, but also the different ways in which He speaks to us, and how to be in the right position in our lives to clearly hear Him whenever He is speaking to us.

A Sanctified Ventriloquist

Ventriloquists are known for being able to "throw their voice." Although they're just one person, they can say things in different ways. We cannot seek to only hear God speak in just one way, for He speaks ("throws His voice") in a variety of different ways. If we are going to truly be listeners and hearers of God's word and voice, then we must understand that God is a sort of sanctified ventriloquist: He can be in one place, and yet put His voice in another place. He can speak through this person, through that person, through actions or inaction, through a woman, through a man, even through a donkey (as in Numbers 22). God speaks in many different ways.

For example, a child learns very early in life that his or her parents don't speak with words alone. Sometimes my momma would speak to me with just a look. I don't know how modern mothers do it with all this "sit in that chair and look at that wall," and "I'm going to give you a time out" stuff. My momma didn't have an *If-you-don't-do-what-I-say-I'll-give-you-a-time-out* ministry. She had a *You-better-get-to-it-or-I'll-take-you-out* ministry. She'd give you a look that made you feel two inches tall, God bless her—and it worked!

Not every student learns in exactly the same way. Some students learn by repeating the information over and over, and they get it. Other students write it down, see it on the page and they get it. Some dramatize it, put some action to it, and that helps them get it. Others visualize the information, turning the words into mental images. Parents learn that one child will get information one way, and another child will get it another way. If we are ever going to learn how to hear God, we must learn that we cannot box Him in to one way and expect Him to only speak that way. He speaks from many different directions, through many different sources and in many different styles. The key is that in order for us to hear Him from any place in our lives, we must be in the right position in our relationship with Him.

Get in Position

Many of us know Exodus 20 as the passage where Moses reveals God's Ten Commandments to the Israelites. But there's a revelation that goes even beyond the giving of the Ten Commandments to the nation, a revelation that comes out of the setting and context in which God spoke the commandments. Exodus 20:18-19 says, "All the people witnessed the thunderings, the lightning flashes, the sound of the trumpet, and the mountain smoking; and when the people saw it, they trembled and stood afar off. Then they said to Moses, 'You speak with us, and we will hear; but let not God speak with us, lest we die.' "

Let me set the scene: It is more than 80 years since Moses had been discovered as an infant floating on the Nile in a basket. By now, he had led the Israelites out of Egypt. He had parted the Red Sea and led them across the sea bed to freedom. And earlier, in Exodus 19:17, he called the people of God to the base of Mount Sinai (at the boundary God had set in Exodus 19:12). God told Moses, "Come to this place and I am going to speak to the people. But when they gather, make sure they are in formation and that they come no farther than the boundary I have set" (see Exod. 19:24). They had all gathered there because almighty Jehovah was going to speak. In other words, the Israelites had learned the importance of being in the right position to hear God.

When the Israelites camped, they did so in a certain position with the Ark of the Covenant in the center of the camp and the people in the formation of the twelve tribes. When the whole nation gathered as one for a particular event or ceremony or to hear God's Word, they would come out of their formation and gather at the designated place. God said, in other words, "If you're going to hear Me, you must be in position. And you must stay in that position or you won't hear Me."

And so, in Exodus 19, after learning the boundaries set for them in order to hear God speak, the Israelites gathered at the base of the mountain (knowing not to get too close to the mountain). In other words, the people got in position, designated by a line that they were instructed not to cross. Come this far and no farther. Get in position and don't cross the line. This passage gives instructions about *where the people are to be*.

Here is what God's saying: "If you're going to hear Me, you must be in position. And stay in that position or you won't hear Me. Don't touch the mountain. Don't climb the mountain. Don't go beyond the barrier I have set for you, so you can hear Me speak." God had anticipated that there would be those who would want to cross the barrier and go and touch the mountain.

There are people who struggle with boundaries—people who want to climb the mountain, examine the mountain and explore the mountain. These people say, "If I can just touch the mountain!" To which God responds, "Don't get too close to the mountain right now, because you'll miss something that I have to say to you." It is important that we learn the boundaries that have been set for us to hear God speak.

Life on the Edge: Our Struggle with Boundaries

One challenge that many of us face in life has to do with boundaries. There's a designated line we are not to cross, but we want to cross it. Or we don't learn where the boundary is, and we cross it. Or we don't listen to instructions, and we cross the line. Then there are people who ask, "Where is that line? I want to get as far outside of that line as I can!" Sadly, however, many people want to know where the line is, not because they're so spiritual, but because they want to see just how close they can get to that line without stepping over. They want to dangle precariously right on the edge, thinking they are living within God's boundaries, yet all the while they're actually living a lifestyle more in choosing with what *they* want, and not what God wants. They live their lives on the edge. It's an attitude of *How close can I get to the line and still represent Jesus?*

An interesting example of this can be seen in the attitudes of young people concerning sexual activities. Young adults today have a saying: "friends with benefits." When I first heard that phrase, I thought it was a good thing. *Good,* I thought, *everybody ought to have some beneficial friends—this is a wonderful thing.* Then my youngest daughter, Jessica, set me straight about it. She said, "No, Daddy. Friends with *benefits*. Get it?" She explained that these kids want to push sexual boundaries with each other. But God says there's a barrier; there are lines that are not to be crossed. And one of those lines is related to holiness. Holiness is not old-fashioned. Holiness means living within the boundaries of a God who commands us: "You shall be holy; for I am holy" (Lev. 11:44-45). Holy is not boring, I promise you. It has far more "benefits" than the world thinks!

Getting Our Attention

In Exodus chapter 20, the Israelites are in position, and God is about to speak to them. And then this happens:

> Now all the people witnessed the thunderings, the lightning flashes, the sound of the trumpet, and the mountain smoking; and when the people saw it, they trembled and stood afar off (Exod. 20:18).

The Israelites got into position to hear God. And then God started speaking the commandments. The sound of His voice was like thunder and lightning and trumpets blowing. The Bible says they backed up and stood afar off. That's not the way they had assumed God was supposed to speak. Whatever He was speaking to them, it didn't sound like their idea of God.

It might well have been like that scene with Moses up on the mountain in the movie *The Ten Commandments* where God speaks, "Thou shalt not..." The sky was flashing, thunder was booming, and every time God said something, there was lightning. When the people witnessed all of the commotion—the thunder and lightning, the sound of the trumpet, the mountain smoking and quaking—they trembled and moved away. They may well have been crying out things like, "Whoa! What in the world is going on up on top of the mountain?!"

The Bible says they got into position, but when God started speaking, the sound of His voice was frightening to them and they backed away. The people said, "If that's the way it is, we're out of here!" It's not always easy to listen to God when He is not saying what we want to hear. What they were hearing was God's firm instructions for believers living on earth. And they did not like the sound of what they were hearing.

It's not always easy to hear when the speaker is saying what you don't want to hear. A while ago, my wife and I were going through some monetary challenges. My wife began to explain to me that there were certain areas where we would have to cut back our spending and what that would cost us in the short run. But everything she said after "what it's going to cost us" I didn't hear because when she got to the things I didn't *want* to hear, I simply tuned her out.

The first rule, if we are going to hear God, is that we must be *in the right position* to hear Him. The second rule is that we must give God our *full focus and attention* in order to hear Him. God spoke in thunder and lightning to get the attention of the Jews. But instead of hearing God's words, the people backed away from God. They had gotten into position. God began to speak. And they got right back out of position because He wasn't saying what they wanted to hear, and He wasn't speaking the way they thought He should speak. They didn't like His words. They didn't like His method. They were afraid. They backed off and told Moses, "Moses, you speak to us yourself and we'll listen. But don't let God speak. Because if God speaks, it will cost us our lives" (see Exod. 20:19). In today's vernacular they might have said it this way: "Hey, Moses, tell you what: why don't you go up and see what God says, with all that thunder and lightning and carrying on up there, and then come on back here and tell us what He said. We don't want to hear it directly from Him, 'cause He sounds pretty mad. So why don't you go up there? If you make it back down here, great. But no need for all of us to go and get wiped out up there."

God spoke in thunder and lightning *to get their attention*, to really impress on them that what He was saying was critical to their existence. But they preferred to have *secondhand information* through somebody else, because they were afraid and didn't want to hear the voice of God Himself. Many people go to church to experience secondhand worship. They seldom participate in the services; they have no engagement in the flow of the gathering. They're content to merely be observers absorbed in the display of the fervent worship of others. This is a bit paradoxical, because those same people would never ask for a secondhand blessing for themselves!

The Secondhand Revelation of Spiritual Pygmies

Too many people are satisfied with what they learn for an hour or so a couple of Sundays each month from their church pulpit. They celebrate and rejoice about how much they "grow" from what they get from the preacher. But what they are hearing (while it's certainly legitimate and no doubt important teaching from the pastor) is *secondhand revelation*. Rather than having the desire to invest the time to get in position to hear God for themselves, these people go to church every now and then and let somebody else tell them what God says.

Too many Christians also go to self-proclaimed "prophets" because they want a shortcut. They'd rather pay a soothsayer to tell them what they think God has to say. Why do people do that? I believe that it's not necessarily that they don't want to know what God has to say. It may be that they're simply not willing to pay the price to get His word for themselves. If the only word you get from God is the word you are spoon-fed from the pulpit once a week or less, then you will never quite be the person who God wants you to be. You won't be as spiritually strong as He wants you to be. You won't gain the level of wisdom He wants for you. You may not be as emotionally mature as He wants you to be. You will never be as victorious as He wants you to be.

God does not speak only through a preacher and only for 1 hour out of the 168 hours in each week. Many times, God has something He wants to tell each of us individually, and He doesn't always want it transferred by somebody else. We must each learn how to also get His word for ourselves. Your spiritual growth will be stunted if you try to thrive off secondhand revelation. You will remain a spiritual pygmy if you only look for somebody else to speak God's word to you. You cannot thumb through the pages of the Word of God, browse the Internet and surf TV channels, hearing what God told somebody else and claiming it for yourself. You can't build a life on a word God may not have meant for you. You can't celebrate somebody else's testimony without having lived the test that they took to get their testimony.

If we don't learn to hear from God for ourselves, we also set ourselves up to fall prey to charlatans who build huge ministries telling people that unless they come to *their* church, hear *their* "spin" on God's word, listen to *their* interpretation of Scripture, then we aren't really hearing from God. There are preachers in pulpits who insinuate that unless God's word comes from *their* mouth, it might not really be a word from God. Following people like that is one of the best ways to create stunted, spiritually anemic people.

One of the motivations of Martin Luther was to bring down the wall of separation between the clergy and the laity. Before the Reformation of the 1500s, laymen had no direct access to the Word of God. Only the priests were allowed to

handle, teach and preach the Word. Luther stood on the principle of the priesthood of believers and was driven by the concept of Christian liberty. One of the liberties God has given the
believer is personal access to the Word. In his book *The Church
in History*, B. K. Kuiper notes that although the average person
did not have access to the Scriptures, "both people and priests
were almost unbelievably ignorant of religious truth. Most
priests were totally unable to preach."[1] Luther's position was
that every believer could—and should—hear the voice of God
through Scripture.

God has something He wants to tell you directly. That's
why you've got to learn how to hear from Him for yourself.
It is valid to come to church to receive a word from the Lord,
but always understand that what you will hear is a corporate
word for that church (hopefully, that's what you will hear).
Often, however, that corporate word will have personal application. But it is the will of God that you also spend one-on-
one time with the Him, allowing Him to speak to you through
His Word.

Hearing God Means Changing

In Exodus 20:19, the people told Moses, "You speak with us,
and we will hear; but let not God speak with us, lest we die."
When you hear from God, there is going to be a cost, a change,
somewhere in your life. Hearing Him without truly changing is
not an option. One of the reasons many of the Israelites didn't
want to hear from God was because they didn't want His word,
His laws and His commands to put a dent in their lifestyle.

The same is true today. Too many people in church every
Sunday don't want to change. They are smorgasbord Christians, picking and choosing what they will follow from among
the selection of what is being presented to them. But when you

have truly heard a word from the throne of God, when God has spoken into your spirit, when He has gotten your attention and He speaks into your mind, you cannot remain the same with the revelation He has given you. You've got to make an adjustment here, a change there, an alteration in your lifestyle, your behavior, your ways. And you will not care who does not like that change in you, because you have heard from God.

It is crucial for us Christians to understand and accept that sometimes God says, "Let it die." Too many of us only claim the life verses and victory passages of the Bible. But if you walk with God long enough, you will find that He reveals to you that there is some stuff in your life that He will not bless. He's not going to anoint it, He's not going to fix it, He's not going to change it. So you'd best *let it die*. If you're not really ready to change, then you don't really want to hear God.

The Bible says the people backed off from God's mountain and stood far off. They cut a deal with Moses: You go on up there and see what God says, and come back and tell us; because if God speaks, it's going to cost us something we aren't ready to pay. One of the reasons so many people are living the same way today as they were last year is because they've only been listening to their preacher. But there's no *power* in a preacher's words (including my own words as a pastor); there is only power in *God's* Word. You can reject a word from the pastor. You can make allowances if the word comes from the minister. You can make excuses such as, "Well, the pastor hasn't exactly got it all that together in his own life. So why should I worry too much about doing it in mine?" Jump on that bandwagon if you want to, but I want to get myself right before God. Because if you hear the word from God, it is going to demand that you make some adjustments. The flipside is that for some people, the worst day of the week is when they are in church, because that's when God will drop something into their spirit and they will

get upset for the rest of the week. Because once God puts something into our mind and spirit, we have a responsibility to do
something about it—and there in our mind it will nag at us until we do (that's one of the functions of the Holy Spirit!). These
people leave church, muttering things like, "I knew I should
have gone to the beach today—I knew it!" or "I should've stayed
home and watched the game!" Because when God speaks, He
demands action, some kind of change, an adjustment somewhere in our lives. And if we refuse to pay attention to what
God is saying to us, He has ways of getting our attention.

To Get Our Attention

Long before God got the attention of the Israelites in Exodus
20, He grabbed Moses' attention in Exodus 3. While Exodus 20
was a corporate word to the Israelites, it began back in Exodus
3 with a personal word to Moses (recall our lesson about *rhema*
words and oracles, from chapter 1).

Here's the scene from Exodus 3: Moses has fled Egypt because he had killed a man and he now goes to Midian. There,
he gets involved with a woman, marries her and starts working
for Jethro, his new father-in-law. One day, as Moses is leading
the flock through the desert on his way to where he thinks is
good pasture, he guides the sheep around the backside of the
mountain. He is then in position to witness an interesting
sight: a burning bush. While it's not unusual for spontaneous
combustion to cause a bush to catch fire when it gets too hot
and dry, the flames are not consuming this bush—and that
really gets his attention.

Moses did not set out that morning to find a flaming bush
that was not burning up. Nor did he have any idea that he was
about to meet his destiny. He was simply going about his every-
day life, looking for pasture as shepherds do, leading the sheep

through wilderness and rough places. But somewhere along the way of his daily activities he came across something that was divinely positioned by Yahweh with an angelic messenger in it that would point Moses to a word directly from God Himself. As Moses arrived at the odd sight of the burning bush, God sent an angel (which means "messenger") who appeared in the bush. A burning bush not being consumed by the flames was the first miracle among many that Moses was going to see in the coming years.

Here's the picture: as Moses is treading down the road, he sees a bush on fire. He says, "I will now turn aside and see this great sight" (Exod. 3:3). In this context, the word "see" means "to look at something for the purpose of gaining information." In other words, "I'll put my attention on it." In the flaming bush is an angel, a messenger sent there by God specifically to communicate something to Moses.

One purpose of miracles is to get our attention. God spoke to Moses through the miracle of a burning bush that was not consumed by the fire. As you look back on your life, you may realize that there were times when you were bopping down the trails of life when God put a little "miracle messenger" blessing in your path that was not just meant to bless you, but was also meant *to get your attention to draw you closer to God*. Perhaps you were so astonished to see the unusual blessing that you marveled at it . . . and kept on going along your merry way, completely missing the revelation God intended for you.

I love the scene toward the end of the movie *The Color Purple* where Shug starts going back to the church and she begins singing, "Maybe God's trying to tell you something." You may be going through fire right now in your life. On the other hand, maybe you are at a place in your life where you are seeing a miraculous manifestation of God. In either case, God is trying to get your attention. He wants you to hear Him.

To Hear Him . . . Take Off Your Shoes

Exodus 3:4 says, "When the LORD saw that he turned aside to look, God called to him from the midst of the bush and said, 'Moses, Moses!' And he said, 'Here I am.'" Only when God saw that Moses had turned aside, did He speak.

An interpretation of that conversation could have gone something like this:

"Moses, you're too high."

"But, Lord," Moses responded, "I'm only wearing sandals."

"Moses, for you, sandals are too high."

"But I'm only up an eighth of an inch on my sandals."

"Even an eighth of an inch is too high, Moses. Don't you know where you're standing? The ground you're standing on is holy ground. Pride cannot enter in here; you cannot be high and mighty here. You stand flat on the dirt. If you'll humble yourself, you'll hear My voice. Now lose the shoes."

Only after Moses gave God his focused attention, took off his sandals as he was told, and then *humbled himself before God*, did God speak the revelation and instructions of Exodus 3 and 4 to him.

It's About Humility

Many of us need to take something off, to adjust something in our lives and humble ourselves, in order for us to hear God speak personal revelation to us. Anything that relies upon our own ingenuity and strength is too high. There are things we will go through that we cannot work our way out of, that we cannot figure our way around, that we cannot fight our own way through. Until God gets our attention, He will not speak to us about these things. But once He gets our attention and we are listening to Him, we are on holy ground. Holy ground is not only where God is; holy ground is where God *speaks*.

What do you need to take off today? What are you standing on that's too high in your life?

"Why, I've been to school and I have a degree."

Too high!

"But I go to church every single Sunday."

Too high!

"I pay my tithes faithfully."

Too high!

"I pray three times every day."

Too high!

In the culture of the times of Exodus, the taking off of shoes was not only an outward indication of humility and subjection to our Lord, it was also a gesture of hospitality. It could be compared to a similar gesture today in the south, where they tell visitors, "Come on in, y'all. Take your shoes off and sit a spell." God also says, "Let me tell you who I am. Take your shoes off. Sit a spell. Let's talk."

God might be telling you right now, "Give Me your attention. Get to a position where you can hear Me speak. Be willing to take off whatever you have to take off, and let's talk." If you want to hear God's voice, you've got to give Him your attention. Holy ground is where He speaks. He wants us to humbly approach Him and say, "Lord, let's talk."

Note

1. B. K. Kuiper, *The Church in History* (Grand Rapids, MI: Eerdmans Publishing Co., 1964), p. 184.

5

The Voice *and* the Storm

Give unto the LORD, O you mighty ones, give unto the LORD glory and strength. Give unto the LORD the glory due to His name; worship the LORD in the beauty of holiness. The voice of the LORD is over the waters; the God of glory thunders; the LORD is over many waters. The voice of the LORD is powerful; the voice of the LORD is full of majesty. The voice of the LORD breaks the cedars, yes, the LORD splinters the cedars of Lebanon. He makes them also skip like a calf, Lebanon and Sirion like a young wild ox. The voice of the LORD divides the flames of fire. The voice of the LORD shakes the wilderness; the LORD shakes the Wilderness of Kadesh. The voice of the LORD makes the deer give birth, and strips the forests bare; and in His temple everyone says, "Glory!" The LORD sat enthroned at the Flood, and the LORD sits as King forever. The LORD will give strength to His people; the LORD will bless His people with peace.

PSALM 29

Psalm 29 has been called the Psalm of the Storm. In this psalm, David poetically and lyrically describes an experience of living life in and through a storm. The psalm is full of storm motifs and descriptions. Seven times in eleven verses in Psalm 29 the phrase "the voice of the Lord" is used. Yet, the emphasis in this psalm is not on the storm itself, but on the voice *and* the storm.

We all go through personal storms throughout our lives. But if we heed God's voice in the storm, then we will develop the kind of faith that responds unquestioningly when Jesus says, "Get out of the boat and follow Me" (see Matt. 14:29). I won't spend time here defining "storm." Most of us can define our own storms of life pretty well. Take a moment and identify or customize your storm in your memory. Your storms may not be the same storms of your neighbor, friends or family. It's alright if you honestly cannot identify a storm in your life; you may never have experienced one . . . *yet*. As my momma used to say, "Keep living"—it will happen!

The psalmist David makes sure that no one is left out when he talks about storms. If you examine the Psalm 29 text carefully, you will discover that David speaks of a storm that is active, moving, changing. Just like when sometimes it's raining on one side of town and sunny on the other, it's not a stagnant storm that David is speaking of. Just because you can't see the storm, doesn't mean that it's not on its way. In Southern California, for example, sometimes when I'm at my office in Inglewood and I call my wife and tell her, "Honey, it is really raining in Inglewood today," she might respond, "Well, the sun is shining over here at our house." Psalm 29 says, "The voice of the LORD is upon the waters. . . . The voice of the LORD breaks the cedars . . . of Lebanon. . . . The voice of the LORD shakes the Wilderness of Kadesh" (vv. 3,5,8). In effect, David is saying that a storm is coming: it's gathering over the waters, moving across the waters, moving over the mountains, and finally, moving over Mount Hermon (which was an inland mountain range also known as Sirion).

Here's the catch: If you're in the mountains, there may be sunshine right now, but there's a storm gathering over the waters *and it's coming your way*. If you're roasting out in the desert, enjoy it, because the sun may be beating down on you now, but a storm is brewing. The message is that every person alive is in one of three places:

1. *Some have just left a storm*. They're praising and worshiping and thanking God because they got through a rough one.

2. *Others are in the midst of a storm.* Things are happening in their lives that are tossing and swirling them. Life feels unstable. They can't quite get their footing, and they're holding on for dear life.

3. *The third group is headed for a storm.* It's coming! . . . It always does.

No matter where you are today, you are either in a storm, you've just left a storm, or you are headed into a storm because that's just the cycle of life. Some folks arrive at church on Sunday having just left a storm. They go to church praising and worshiping and thanking God that—*hallelujah!*—they just got through a rough one. Others go to church on Sunday in the midst of a storm. Things are going on in their lives that are causing them great turmoil. Howling winds, thrashing debris, blustery skies. Things are unstable. They're holding on to anything and everything nearby because they are going *through it.* They may be dressed up all nice, sitting in the pew with a pleasant look on their face, but their eyes show it: things are rough. I can't even tell you about some of the storms I've been through. Some storms are so intimate and personal that we can't even tell our friends about them. But there is hope. Psalm 29:3 says, "The voice of the Lord is over the waters." This is very important. *The voice of the Lord* means "God speaks." If you've ever been in an airplane and looked down over dark clouds below as the plane begins to descend into them, you've had a God's-eye view of what's ahead of you, while the voice of the Lord remains above you and the plane as it makes its way toward the thunderclouds. Psalm 29:10 says, "The LORD sat enthroned at the Flood." The storm is raging over you, but God is speaking from above the storm. The position of being "enthroned" and "sitting above" symbolizes that He *reigns above;* He is reigning from on high. One version says "the LORD sitteth" (*KJV*). He has taken position—the position of being enthroned and sitting over it all.

Let's settle this right now: No matter what your storm is, God is King over that storm. He reigns over the storm. He still sits on the throne. He is still in charge. He is still God—the same yesterday, today and tomorrow. God was on the throne before the storm began, He's on the throne while the storm is raging, and He will be on the throne when the storm has passed. Through it all, no matter what storm you are facing or are deep in the throes of, it is important to keep in mind that Christ reigns over *all* storms. More importantly, He is right there with you as you go through the storm.

Christ in the Storm

He said to them, "Let us cross over to the other side." . . .
And a great windstorm arose, and the waves beat into the boat,
so that it was already filling.
MARK 4:35,37

At the conclusion of Mark 4, after a long day of preaching, Jesus tells the disciples to get in a boat so they can go over to the other side of the Sea of Galilee. But a storm begins raging during their journey. The waves are tossing, churning, thumping, and the small boat starts taking on water. One of them cries out, "Lord, the waves are so great and the boat is so small!" *The stuff that's coming against me is so big I can't handle it! I'm about to be overtaken by this!* Not only is a storm raging, but they're also in imminent danger of being swamped.

The tempest is raging, the waves are tossing high and the sky is dark. No shelter or help is nigh. Then, in the midst of the storm, as the boat is filling with water and is about to go down, in verse 38, somebody remembers: Jesus is on-board! He's on a pillow . . . in the middle of a raging storm . . . *asleep!* The text makes a point to tell us that He's asleep *on a pillow.* He's off into sleepy land, snoozing away in the middle of a raging storm. (I could write an entire book about that scenario alone!)

When it looks like your boat is about to go under, that's a pretty good time to remember that Jesus is on-board. When it looks like your life is sinking, when you're about to succumb to the waves of oppression trying to overtake you, it's a perfect time to remember that Jesus is on-board. You're already in a lifeboat: Jesus is there! Storms move. Sometimes it's raining and storming out in the middle of the sea, but it's dry on the shore. If I had a choice, I'd rather be in the boat in the storm with Jesus than on the sunny shore all by myself. The lesson is that whatever storms you are going through, you're not going through them all alone.

Back to Mark 4:38. The tempest is raging, the waves are tossing, the sky is dark. No shelter or help is nigh. Then the disciples remember that Jesus is on-board, and they awake Him and say, "Teacher, do You not care that we are perishing?" *How can You lay there asleep when the angry sea is threatening to make of itself a grave for us! Help!*

In verse 39, Jesus stands. He raises His hand to the storm (because even the wind and the waves obey His will), and He commands them, "Peace, be still!" And the wind ceases, and there is a great calm. Sometimes we all just need Jesus to speak to our storm and say, "QUIET! Peace, be still."

Notice that Jesus didn't speak to the disciples; He spoke to *the storm.* Why would He speak to the storm? Remember, when they had departed for the other side, Jesus said to the disciples, "Let's go over . . ." The boat was taking on water, which means they were in danger of going under. But here is Jesus saying—from inside the sinking boat, no less—*let's go over.* When God has given you a destiny to go over, He speaks to anything that would cause you

Weapons: Alcohol doubt
against me   Money

to go under because no matter what opposition comes against you, no matter how much water your boat of life is taking on, when God has destined you to arrive in your destiny, the very devil in hell cannot cause you to go under. All the weapons designed to stop you or block you shall be formed, but no weapon that is formed against you shall prosper (see Isa. 54:17).

When God says, "Go over," you can't go under; you're going over. You thought you were about to go under. You thought this thing that came against you was going to get you down. You thought you would not make it through. But no matter the opposition you face, when God has destined you to get to the other side, His voice speaks to your storm and says, "Peace, be still!" You're going over. He speaks to *the storm* you are in, He speaks to *you* in that storm and He speaks to the storm that is *in you*.

One of the great voices of gospel music in the African American tradition was the late Reverend James Cleveland. Reverend Cleveland popularized the kind of music sung on Sunday mornings in black churches with innovation and musical creativity that became the foundation of today's praise and worship genre. He became a gospel legend through his release of a song that tells the story we just examined in the fourth chapter of Mark. Few people are aware that there are several verses to the popular song "Peace Be Still."

Cleveland summarizes and encapsulates the essence of the voice of God in our storms with this inspirational message that sets to music the dialogue between Jesus and the disciples (or maybe the dialogue *we* have with the Lord when we are in our storms!). He musically pictures the disciples frantically arousing a sleeping Jesus with the pronouncement of impending doom on a raging sea. The sky is blackened, the winds are raging and the sea is tossing the little boat back and forth like a ping-pong ball. They are amazed at what they imply is not only an inopportune time for a nap, but the seemingly lack of concern on the part of the Master. They wonder if He knows and more importantly, if He really cares that they face a grave in the unruly deep. With both startling words set to the tune of a flowing wavelike melody line and broad majestic chordal progressions, Jesus declares His mastery over the wind and the waves. Cleveland paints a musically artistic picture of our Lord stepping to the helm of the ship, pronouncing the benediction on the stormy sea with the command, "Peace! Be Still!" Ahhh. What a voice. It is a voice that can calm the storms you face, speak peace to your fear-filled soul, and direct you to the safety and security of solid ground!

It's better to be in the storm with Jesus than on the shore in the sunshine without Him. He speaks in the storms of life. He speaks peace. Now let's take a look at the comparative physiology of the storm path: the waters, the desert (wilderness) and the cedars (mountains).

The Waters: Separation from God

The voice of the LORD is over the waters;
the God of glory thunders; the LORD is over many waters.
PSALM 29:3

In this passage, "the waters" symbolize being away from God. It represents the "natural man" whose heart is turned away from God. When the Bible says the Lord speaks to the waters, I believe it means He speaks to those who are away from Him; people whose lives are being lived contrary to the ways of their Creator. Isaiah 23:12, "Arise, cross over to Cyprus; there also you will have no rest," characterizes this condition of separation from God as *having no rest*. In fact, when we choose to live life apart from God, it is like being on a raging sea. It is impossible to get rest!

Isaiah 23:12 speaks of those times in our lives when we are
so far from God that we are unfulfilled even in the face of success and accomplishment. There are things in our life that
should fulfill us, but "no rest" means no fulfillment. It's the
idea of a person who has material possessions but possesses no
true peace. One who has success, but lacks substance. It's what
is lacking in the midnight hour after the lights are off and the
crowds are gone. It symbolizes the successful person who has
climbed the ladder, acquired many possessions, is doing well,
but if the truth were told, he or she is actually living proof of the
words of Augustine: "We were made for Thee and our soul find-
eth no rest till we rest in Thee."

These people lack fulfillment by the things of this world.
They've tried everything else; they've been around the horn and
now they hear the voice of God, speaking to their emptiness in
the storm of their life. These are people who are worldly successful, but are living in the world without a heavenly God. "No
rest" implies *constantly moving, constantly on the go*. They run after *things*, and when they get them, they're not fulfilled, so they
run after other things. These people remain seemingly compul-
sively obsessed with getting that which never fulfills them.

The world's goal is to give you success and pleasure without
God. The world is not concerned about you being successful as
long as that success does not include or depend upon God. If
you can get success without God, then the world has won. God
wants you to know that even though there may be a semblance
of success, there is no fulfillment with any type of success that
comes apart from Him. In Matthew 16:26, Jesus raises the question that challenges worldly success that costs you your soul. Is
success *really* successful if you have to forfeit eternal life to get
it? In Ecclesiastes 1:2, Solomon questions the things that feed
our vanity, and he concludes that it is "nothing but smoke"
(*THE MESSAGE*).

you have not because you ask) not.

The Desert: The Storm Within

The voice of the LORD shakes the desert;
the LORD shakes the Desert of Kadesh.

PSALM 29:8, *NIV*

It's one thing to speak to the storm we are in (and praise the Lord, He speaks to us in that storm), but it's another thing when the storm is *in you*. Deep down inside many people, there's a raging storm consuming them.

James 1:6-8 says, "He who doubts is like a wave of the sea driven and tossed by the wind. For let not that man suppose that he will receive anything from the Lord; he is a double-minded man, unstable in all his ways." The storm within is storm of doubt. "Should I do this, or should I do that?" It speaks of one who is wavering back and forth. "Should I go here, or should I go there?" These are people who don't know what in the world they should do or how to even begin trying to figure that out. They're so paralyzed with indecision that they end up doing nothing and going nowhere. They are victims of the paralysis of analysis. They're treading water. Spinning their wheels. Two steps forward, three steps back.

The Cedars: Strength in the Storm

The voice of the LORD breaks the cedars, yes, the LORD
splinters the cedars of Lebanon.

PSALM 29:5

Cedar is wood that was used in the construction of the temple. "The cedars of Lebanon" symbolize the people of God, righteous ones who know and love the Lord, and yet they are in a storm. These "cedars" are people who are listening to hear a word from God. These are the people of God who are in the midst of a storm but are listening for God's voice because they recognize that God would not allow them to go into a storm alone.

It is interesting to note that when the psalmist talks about speaking *over the waters* (referring to people who are away from God), the phrase "the voice of the Lord" appears three times. In other words, God speaks three times to those who are away from Him. However, when it comes to *the cedars of Lebanon* (those who are not away from God, but are experiencing rough times), it uses that phrase only one time. This is because God only has to speak to the cedars one time because these are people who only have to be told once. They have gotten to a point in their walk with God where He doesn't have to keep repeating Himself to them. These are people who are so spiritually sensitive that when God says it, they get it and they do it. They recognize that they're in a hard place, they're in a storm, they're facing a challenge, but they simply want to know, "Lord, I'm in a rough spot here. What would You have me do? Speak but a word, Lord, and I'll do it. You won't have to tell me twice."

With some people, God has been telling them the same thing for the last 5 years, 10 years, 20 years because they haven't done it yet. They haven't gotten it into their heads yet, and they aren't hearing His voice yet. They're still not doing what He tells them to do, and they're still finding excuses not to change. Some people are just hardheads. The goal for all Christians is to get to a point where God doesn't have to keep repeating instructions, admonitions and warnings to us.

Times of Testing

When the psalm talks about the voice of the Lord over the cedars of Lebanon, it speaks of the people of God who are in a time of testing. You cannot tell the strength of something until it has been tested. The strength of the cedars that were used to build part of the Temple were supposed to withstand storms. But you will never know whether you can withstand a storm until you go through one.

Many people look good in church. But until they are truly tested in the storms of life, they won't really know how strong they are. God allows the unexpected to happen so He can see if we really trust Him like we said we did before the storm came crashing in. Some people talk about how holy they are and how righteous they behave (and praise the Lord, that's how they should be), but they just haven't been tested the right way yet. Sometimes, people are holy by default because they haven't had any offers, stresses or blessings that test them. It is in the times of testing that the Lord speaks, and our strength is tried. Anybody can trust Him in the sunshine, but it's when the storm is so awful that it bends the cedar trees that our faith is fully revealed.

One of the disappointing, and sometimes discouraging, things about being a pastor and walking with people in their relationship with the Lord is seeing how they handle the storms of life. It often appears that God has something in common with us: we both have fair-weather friends. I have seen people come, and I have seen them go. I fight being cynical when I see the fervency of some worshipers when the sun is shining. However, all too often, when the storms of life roll in, many people roll out. Many of us are only one storm away from turning from the Lord. Much of the contemporary theology in our culture seems to imply that there is a storm-exclusion clause in our salvation contract (maybe they haven't read John 16:33 yet!).

Nowadays, we find out about upcoming storms through meteorologists. Meteorologists use the Saffir-Simpson Hurricane Scale, which measures the strength of the winds of a hurricane. The highest category, the one with the strongest winds, is a category 5, which has winds of more than 155 miles per hour. In late August 2005, Hurricane Katrina reached a Category 5, with winds of 175 miles per hour. As you may recall, it paralyzed the entire Gulf Coast area of America; its effects are still being felt. Even as you read these words, thousands of lives have yet to recover from Hurricane Katrina. All because of a storm. As tragic and sad as this is in the natural world, it raises an interesting and introspective spiritual query for you to consider: How strong does a storm have to be to halt your life? What category of storm will cease your spiritual progress, stunt your spiritual growth and stop your spiritual journey?

Hebrews 12:26-27 warns believers that the Lord will shake everything that can be shaken so that when He gets through shaking, the only thing left is what cannot be shaken: your *faith*. The day is going to come where there's going to be a whole lot of shaking going on, just to see what could not be shaken loose. It is when God desires to show you how strong you thought you were. It's when something comes into your life that (before it arrived) you were confident you could handle. And then it hit you—and you never expected it to knock you like that. You considered the possibilities, but when it hit, it shook you more than you thought it would. You thought you had big faith, but something happened in the earth realm that caught you so off guard that when it hit you, you didn't understand why you were tripping up and going through such a hard time with it.

When the unexpected occurs, God wants to see if you really do trust Him like you claimed you did before the storm arose. Anybody can trust Him when the bank account is full, the family is healthy and the job is going fine. But when you get out there and the world slaps you upside your head with things you weren't expecting, that's when you need to hear a word from God. It's when you train your child up in the way they should go: you took them to Sunday school, you took them to the choir, you took them to the church youth activities. But then something happens in the midnight hour when your daughter is on a date and the fellow is taking advantage of her and you aren't there and there's not a thing you can do. Things like that will throw a parent off—I don't care how much they say they love Jesus. When you've done your absolute best to raise your child in the training and admonition of the Lord and that child goes south on you and ends up in the far country and has a fall and you can't kiss it and make it better. It's in dark hours like those when you had better listen for a word from God. It's when that stuff hits you and throws you off. It's not because you don't love Jesus and aren't saved and sanctified; it's just because those storms will rise up unexpectedly and shake your faith. It happens to all of us.

Searching for God in the Disaster

Several years ago my wife and I brought a young lady from Los Angeles to live with us as our daughter. I had met her while speaking at a youth leadership conference when she was 16 years old. True to the trend in South African township schools, she was just over 20 when she finally graduated from high school. We had made arrangements for her to come to America and go to college, and we had prepared her a room in our home. We anticipated her arrival with great joy. Two months before she was to arrive in America, she called us, weeping. She had been working in downtown Johannesburg and was waiting for a taxi to take her back to Kwa-Tema, the township where she lived. A man approached her and forced her into a dark street away from the taxi area. And he raped her.

She called me after being taken to the hospital. I don't think I can adequately express the intense pain in my gut and the inexpressible frustration I felt talking to my daughter, hearing her recount the ordeal that would change her life. I wanted so much to go there, to hold her, to comfort her, to tell her it was going to be all right, to tell her I loved her. She was on the other side of the world, and I was helplessly bound in the isolation of the miles between us. This man had viciously raped this young lady. I don't know if it was more the mind of a parent or the mind of a man that pressed my mental rewind and fast-forward buttons at the same time, bombarding my thoughts with graphic images of my child being brutalized by a savage. The *whys* kept racing through my mind: Why, Lord? Why did this happen? Why wasn't I there? Why did God allow this? Why didn't God stop it? Why would You let him do that to her? Why? Why?! *Why?!* I was in a storm!

I wish I could tell you that I weathered that storm with high-flying spiritual colors, like a cedar of Lebanon. But the storm was only starting. When my daughter was taken to the hospital after the rape, she had to undergo a test for HIV, the virus that causes AIDS.[1] The nurse who did her examination told her she was negative, and advised her to get tested every 6 months, explaining that the virus can remain dormant for up to 10 years.

It was about nine years later that my daughter discovered that she had AIDS. In fact, she found out because she was having complications with a pregnancy and had a miscarriage. A year later, she died.

My boat capsized in that storm. I should have some testimony for you of unwavering faith as I stood tall in the demonic winds of my personal storm . . . but I don't. I was shaken! I didn't understand. There was something terribly wrong with traveling on a plane for almost 24 hours to attend a funeral for my daughter, whose body was a mere skeleton of her former self after a tragic bout with a deadly disease. Where was God in *that* storm?

I know this book is supposed to be about hearing God over the cacophony of the soundtrack of the world, and I know I should fill these pages with storm success stories, but I want you to understand the reality of the muffled voice of God during the raging Katrinas of life that seem to be off the category scale when you are either drifting in a wind-tossed catastrophe or experiencing the deafening silence of nothingness in your search for answers, rhyme or reason. The best I can tell you is that *I did not turn from God.* I did "look away," but I didn't "turn away." Not because I am so spiritual, but because my spirit echoed the frustrated faith of Peter in John 6:68: Where else could I go?

I felt like Job. I looked for God in this disaster and could not find Him. I strained to hear His voice, but the deafening bellow of my questioning pain smothered His evidently still, small voice. I did look away, but I did not turn away. I had no place else to go. I had no other refuge. I had no other resting place. I realized I sounded like the psalmist, in spite of myself. Over and over and over, in the middle of the loneliness of the nights, in the darkness of my own empty questions, I found myself repeating an embarrassingly simplistic prayer: *Have mercy, Lord. Have mercy, Lord. Have mercy, Lord. Have mercy, Lord.* Without realizing it, I guess my soul was gasping with the words of Psalm 57:1, "Be merciful unto me, O God, be merciful unto me: for my soul trusteth in thee: yea, in the shadow of thy wings will I make my refuge, until these calamities be overpast" (*KJV*). I wasn't trying to be scriptural or spiritual or godly or pious. I hurt, I was in pain, I was drowning in the sea of my own answerless questions. *Have mercy on me, Lord.*

I still struggle with the loss of my daughter. Especially to such a violent and senseless end to a life that was only just beginning. My faith was shaken. But not shaken loose!

Thy Will Be Done

Do you have the kind of faith that cannot be shaken? Do you have that kind of love that cannot be loosened, even when a

storm rises up unexpectedly? The testing does not mean that
God has abandoned you. It merely means that *it's your turn for
some testing.* Not because you don't love Jesus, not because God is
mad at you, not because you're being punished, but just because
it's simply *your time.*

"But why me, God?" many people moan. Well, why *not* you?
What makes you so special that you should not be tested? Cedars of
Lebanon are believers, strong pillars of the Kingdom. Job went
through this type of testing—*and then some.* Even Jesus had to go
through testing. He went through Calvary (top that one!). He passed
the test with four small but mighty words: "Thy will be done."

These times of testing reveal how much faith you really have
when facing the realities and challenges of real life. Big storms
and little storms both test the size of our faith. Couples who must
navigate their relationship through the choppy waters of an enduring commitment may experience the paradox of celebrating
an anniversary while sitting at the kitchen table looking for more
corners to cut in light of an uncontrollable economic downturn
on one hand and undisciplined spending on the other hand.
Times like that are when you need to go back to the "until death
do us part" portion of your marriage vows. That's what you said
then. In the bad times, go back and recall the good times; they'll
come again. But for now, it's the bad time. You told your wife or
husband, "Through sunshine or rain, baby." Well, it's raining bill
collectors all over the place now. The bad time has arrived. Life is
throwing stuff at your marriage unexpectedly and leaks are
springing left and right, repo men are appearing at odd hours,
threatening letters are arriving, bankruptcy is calling. It does not
mean God has abandoned you! It only means that it's your turn.
Deal with it like a Christian. God won't leave you to drown. God
can speak to you in the storm.

Matthew 14:25 recounts another time when Peter and the
others were in a boat on the sea. Waves started rolling up on

them. But this time, Jesus was not in the boat. The storm was raging, the winds were blowing, and the waves were promising to swamp them. They thought they were going under. In desperation they looked out on the horizon . . . and there came a strange figure, walking on the water: Jesus!—seemingly taking a casual stroll in the middle of a storm—*on top of the raging sea*, no less! Jesus just doesn't seem to think that storms are all that much to get excited about, does He? There He comes, padding along on the water in the middle of a tempest. Boat full of disciples, full of cedars, full of praisers, full of the living God, full of those who are saved, sanctified and filled with the precious Holy Ghost. And Jesus says to them, "You've got so much faith, get on out of the boat. Come on—follow Me. You got that kind of faith? Let's go."

Jesus is enthroned on the storm. He's not under the storm; He's walking on top of it. Let me tell you something in the words of the title of John Ortberg's classic book: If you want to walk on water, you've got to get out of the boat. You've got to get out of that boat, baby! Do not fear. Jesus commands all storms.

Jesus said, "Don't be afraid. It's Me."

Peter said, "If that's You, then command me to come."

"Come on," Jesus responded. He only called him once. *You say you've got so much faith? Then get on out of that boat and come.*

Peter got out, and he walked on the water in the middle of a storm with Jesus.

All I want to know in my storms is this: *Is God in this storm?* I don't care what's going on around me. If I ever get the idea that God is in it, then here I come. I'm coming through hell, Lord. I'm coming through high water, Father. I'm coming through the haters, Jesus. I'm coming through the doubters, my God. I'm coming through the storm with *You*, Jesus!

What boat is God telling you to get out of? You will never become all that God wants you to be in the boat you're in. That boat is not strong enough, that boat is not holy enough, that boat is not rigid enough. And sometimes, where God wants to take you, there are folks in your boat who can't go with you. You've got to say to them, "This boat don't float. I'm out of here. I can't take this anymore. I'm going with Jesus."

The devil doesn't want us deciding to follow the voice of God. The devil wants us mired in the paralysis of analysis. He wants us so obsessed with trying to figure things out that we wind up becoming unstable, immobile and unable to move forward because we're so stuck trying to analyze where we are. Getting yourself out of that paralysis of analysis takes one simple choice: *stop doubting!* Make a decision to trust God. Tell Him, "If this is right, Lord, I praise You. And if it's wrong, You will have to correct it because I'm going to follow Your word no matter what. I'm not going to stay stuck here."

> He who doubts is like a wave of the sea driven and tossed by the wind (Jas. 1:6).

Doubters waver because of the storm within them. But God speaks and says, "That's enough. No more wind, no more waves. Sit down, storm. Lay down, waves. That's enough. She's been through enough. He's been through enough."

If you've had enough, tell the Lord, "Speak to my storm, Lord, because I've had enough."

Trust the Voice of Peace

The LORD will give strength to His people;
the LORD will bless His people with peace.
PSALM 29:11

When God speaks, He releases two things: strength and peace. What did He say when He spoke to the storm? He said, "Peace." What does He say to us in the midst of our storms? He says,

"Peace." When He speaks, He gives strength, and then He blesses us with peace. In John 14:27, Jesus said, "Peace I leave with you, My peace I give to you; not as the world gives do I give to you. Let not your heart be troubled, neither let it be afraid." In Philippians 4:7, Paul said, "The peace of God, which surpasses all understanding, will guard your hearts and minds through Christ Jesus."

There will be people around you who know what you're going through and can't understand how you're dealing with it with such grace and calm. They're close enough to you to know your travails. They know something about the trials, about the storms, about the winds and waves pounding your life. And when you didn't know you could make it through another day and go through another round, you did. Some people who have gone through what you went through wouldn't still be going to church, wouldn't still be praising God, and wouldn't still be worshiping the Lord. But you are. You're a cedar, an example to them all that the storm within can be quelled by simple choice: *trust God*. Becoming a cedar of Leb-anon begins with a *desire* to hear God's voice, and a choice to *trust* what He says. You know you are there not just when folks look at you and they don't understand why you have peace, but when *you* look at you and *you* don't understand why you have such peace. Peace not as the world gives, but peace that passes all understanding (see Phil. 4:7). Peace that overtakes you when just yesterday you didn't think you were going to make it to another day. Or last night when you didn't know you could make it through the night. Or last year when you didn't know if you could make it through all the devil threw at you. But look at you now: After all you've been through, you're still standing.

God's voice is what gets you through the storm. It's important to remind yourself, "I'm still here. I'm still praising. I've still got a 'hallelujah' on my lips and in my heart. I still have a

'Thank You, Jesus.' I still have a 'Praise the Lord.' I don't understand it, but I'm going to praise Him. I'm going to bless His
holy name. I will bless the Lord at all times, and His praise shall
continually be in my mouth."

One of the traditions in my home church, Mt. Zion Missionary Baptist Church in East St. Louis, Illinois, was first Sunday
night communion testimony service. This was a period at the
beginning of the service much like an open-mic gathering where
anyone could stand and give a personal testimony of something
the Lord had done in their lives (hopefully, since the last first
Sunday, but something that often took us back to the "red clay
hills of Mississippi," as one of the deacons would say—though
I'm not sure there are red clay hills in Mississippi!). Most of the
old saints would stand and introduce their testimony with a
song. (Although I remember many of them to this day, I must
admit I really didn't understand the spiritual significance of
some of the messages of the songs.) One of the regular songs on
the testimony top 10 list that captured the reality of life in the
storm was written by Thomas A. Dorsey. In the picturesque, creative style that came to characterize this composer/musician
known as "the Father of Gospel," Dorsey paints a musical picture of both the havoc and hope of the storms of life:

> *Like a ship that's tossed and driven, battered by an angry sea;*
> *When the storms of life are raging, and their fury falls on me.*
> *I wonder what I have done, that makes this race so hard to run;*
> *Then I say to my soul, take courage, the Lord will make a way somehow.*
> THOMAS DORSEY, "THE LORD WILL MAKE A WAY SOMEHOW"

Note
  1. South Africa has the highest incidence of AIDS-infested people in the entire world.
  According to a 2009 Human Sciences Research Council report, nearly one in three
  women from the age of 25 to 29, and over a quarter of men between 30 and 34, are
  living with HIV.

6

Speak to Me, Lord

(Now Samuel did not yet know the LORD, nor was the word of the LORD yet revealed to him.) And the LORD called Samuel again the third time. So he arose and went to Eli, and said, "Here I am, for you did call me." Then Eli perceived that the LORD had called the boy.

1 SAMUEL 3:7-8

In an earlier chapter, we touched briefly on the passage above. Let me set the scene for these two verses: This is the third time that the Lord had spoken to Samuel, who was a boy at the time. The first two times, upon hearing the voice, Samuel went to Eli the priest and said, "Here I am, for you called me" (1 Sam. 3:5-6). Eli answered, in effect, "Nope. Wasn't me. Go on back to bed."

Then, the third time God called Samuel, again thinking that Eli had called him, Samuel went to the priest and said, "Here I am, for you did call me" (v. 8).

Then Eli perceived that it was the Lord who had been calling the boy. So Eli told Samuel, "Go and lie down, and if he calls you, say, 'Speak, LORD, for your servant is listening.'"

So Samuel went and laid down on his bed, and sure enough, "the LORD came and stood there, calling as at the other times, 'Samuel! Samuel!' Then Samuel said, 'Speak, for your servant is listening'" (see vv. 8-10).

Several points are revealed in the text:

1. Samuel was a young man. He was not a baby, nor was he a little child. The Hebrew word used to refer

to Samuel, *na'ar*, indicates a young man, a lad, a youth. He was at least a teenager. Eli was what we might call Samuel's mentor, his teacher. Samuel served in the temple under the tutelage of Eli.

2. The Bible explains with great clarity that Samuel did not yet know the Lord. So, here was God, *calling someone who did not know Him* (which is important to note), and yet, He was calling him.

3. Samuel also did not know, nor did he recognize, the voice of God. God had called Samuel several times, and each time he mistook the voice of God for Eli the priest.

4. Eli helped young Samuel know that the voice of God was calling him, and he told him how to respond.

As the text shows with young Samuel, not all of us will always know when God is speaking to us. Many of us could probably look back over our lives and see that at some points along the way, God was speaking to us, but we didn't realize it was Him at the time. God was speaking to young Samuel, yet Samuel had no clue that it was God who was speaking. Even though God had called to him at least three times, Samuel assumed that it was someone else; he thought it was Eli.

The text is very clear in pointing out that Samuel did not yet know the Lord. This illustrates the fact that God spoke to every single saved person *before* they knew Him (before they were "saved")—*and they heard His voice.* Therefore, if you know the Lord as your Savior, then you too have heard Him speak to you at least once: He called to you even before you knew Him, and you said *yes* to His call. That may clash against some people's theology, but it is important for every Christian to know. He has spoken directly and personally to each of us before we became a Christian. Many of us remember well the moment that happened. I was 10 years old when I first realized God was speaking to me, and without all of the additional, optional theological accessories, I accepted Jesus Christ as my Savior. My mother died in 2009 at the age of 94, but she would often talk about hearing the Lord speak to her down by the banks of the Mississippi creek where she was baptized. She never forgot it, and she never stopped talking about it.

It is easy to assume that God only speaks to others. But the truth is, God speaks to each of us. If you get nothing else out of this book, then get this: God wants you to know that *He speaks to you*. We will never grow in our relationship with the Lord and become the man or woman God wants us to be until we realize and begin to walk in the truth that God speaks to us. We've all heard about people to whom God spoke—and most of us are comfortable agreeing that God did indeed speak to them. But God speaks to *you*, too. And if He did once, then He can do it again, at any time.

Equally crucial to learning how to recognize God's voice is to *respond* when He calls. Knowing His voice and responding takes willingness to initiate (Samuel followed Eli's instructions that he speak to God next time he heard God's voice) and takes relationship to sustain (after responding to God, Samuel began a decades-long relationship with God that included Samuel becoming the priest who appointed Saul as Israel's first king, David as the second king, and countless conversations with God throughout his life).

Many Ways!

So, what are the ways in which God speaks to us? In *Hearing God*, Dallas Willard's masterpiece on this subject, Willard writes, "God could certainly *determine* the course of our lives by manipulating

our thoughts and feelings or by arranging external circumstances—what is often called the 'closing' and 'opening' of
doors in the 'sovereign will' of God. But He can and does also
guide us by *addressing* us. . . . God addresses us in various ways:
in dreams, visions, and voices; through the Bible and extraordinary events; and so forth."[1] Let's examine a few of the ways.

Through Phenomena and His Voice

Sometimes in the Bible, God speaks through supernatural phenomenon and His voice. This is where there is first a revelation
of a phenomenon, and then God speaks. An example would be
when God spoke to Moses out of the burning bush. Or when
He spoke to Israel from out of the cloud at the base of the
mountain in Exodus 20. Or from the whirlwind in Ezekiel 1.
Or when Jesus was baptized and the heavens opened and the
voice of God announced, "This is My beloved Son, in whom I
am well pleased" in Matthew, Mark and Luke.

Through Dreams and Visions

There are people in the Bible who had dreams in which God
spoke to them, and there are those who saw visions wherein
God spoke to them. In many cases, visions are not dreams, and
dreams are not visions. For the most part, it seems that dreams
are often more difficult to interpret, whereas visions are often
more clear.

Joel 2:28 states that in the latter days God will pour out
His spirit and old men shall dream dreams and young men
shall see visions. Acts 10 tells of when Peter saw the vision of
heaven opening and something like a large sheet being let
down to earth by its four corners, containing all kinds of four-
footed animals, reptiles and birds (the message of which was
that God was telling Peter he should not call Gentiles impure
or unclean).

When I was in London a while ago, a friend of mine told me that she had a vision of her son-in-law dying. When she told her son-in-law about the dream, he revealed to her that he was on drugs. She responded, "You're going to kill yourself." That was a wakeup call for him—her vision turned his life around.

Through Angels

Sometimes God speaks through angels. In Genesis 18 and 19 there were angels who spoke. There are situations where the Bible talks about "the army of the Lord," which were often angels. There are people who have said they have seen Christophanies, which are manifestations of Christ or angels. There are dozens of passages throughout the Bible where God speaks through angels who appear to someone. Two instances were when the archangel Gabriel talked to Elizabeth and then to Mary about the births of John and Jesus. There are, of course, many other examples of angels sent by God to speak His word to people here on earth (see Exod. 3:2; Judg. 6:11-17; 13:3-5; Matt. 1:20; Luke 1:26-38; 2:8-20).

I know people who say they went through things, and there was a mysterious person there who helped them through whatever was happening at the time. One man told me that if not for a stranger who appeared in front of him saying, "Go this way," there would have been a car accident; and when he turned around to thank the person, the person had vanished. Was that an angel? I don't know. Was it an apparition? I don't know. Was it a figment of their imagination? I don't know. But he said that whatever or whoever it was, it saved his life.

In an Audible Voice

Throughout biblical history, God often speaks in an audible voice as He did to Adam and Eve, Noah, Abraham, Jacob, Solomon, Jonah, Samuel, and many others. It's very clear in 1 Samuel

3, for instance, that what God spoke to Samuel was audible because the text repeats over and over that Samuel heard the voice. He didn't understand it, he didn't recognize it, he didn't know it was God until Eli told him, but he heard the voice.

I know a few people who have heard an audible voice of God. I have always wondered what His voice sounds like. Is it deep? Is it flowing or booming or curt or soft? Maybe He sounds like His voice was portrayed in the movie *The Ten Commandments* when Charlton Heston said in that commanding, authoritative voice, "Moses, stretch out your staff!"

I have never heard God's audible voice, but I think it would be amazing. The closest and most vivid time that I "heard" God's voice was at a critical crossroads in my life. After having failed miserably at marriage as a young man, my life drifted in and out of the valley of deep depression. Then one Sunday night, I went for coffee with a friend of mine. She was supposed to have had dinner with the guy she was dating at the time, but he had stood her up (the guy was a real loser!). She and I had been friends for years. In fact, we met while in junior high school in East St. Louis. Her family attended a church that was in fellowship with the church where I served as organist (I was about 15 or 16 years old at the time). We had known each other through high school and college, and had always shared a purely platonic friendship (she was actually more like a sister to me). When she came to Los Angeles after graduating from Southern Illinois University, I was the only person she knew. I promised her parents that I would look out for her, and I'd never let her go hungry. This particular Sunday night was supposed to be a little social get-together between two old friends. And it was just that. After spending some brief time talking about what a dog her ex-boyfriend had turned out to be, I took her to her home and gave her the proverbial peck on the cheek, appropriately placed by a good friend.

On my way home, I stopped at a stop sign two blocks from her apartment. It was the corner of Third and Western. Over the soft rhythms of a soulful song on KGFJ Radio, I "heard" what I acknowledged to be the voice of God. Now, as I said, it wasn't audible, but I can tell you it was as clearly spoken in my spirit as the voice that I heard as a boy of 10 years old calling me to salvation. At that stop sign at the corner of Third and Western, the voice said to me, "What you have been looking for all of your life has been under your nose for 12 years." Okay, okay. I know that's not the verbiage of the voice out of the burning bush or the pillar of cloud or the sound of heaven declaring, "This is My Beloved Son," but I heard that voice in my spirit. I know my experience was a bit more colloquial than those Bible events, but now, after almost 34 years of marriage to that very woman, trust me—I declare unto you that I heard the voice of God! And the sound was sweet.

Objectively and Subjectively

Those are four of the ways in which God speaks. The two most common methods He uses to speak to us, however, are *objectively* and *subjectively*. Let's take a look at each of them.

Objectively

God speaks to us through other human beings. One example of this is when Moses spoke the word of God to the Hebrews in the wilderness. In Deuteronomy 18:18, God told the people through Moses, "I will raise up for them a prophet like you from among their brothers; *I will put my words in his mouth*, and he will tell them everything I command him" (*NIV; emphasis added*).

In Exodus, when God instructed Moses that he was to go to Pharaoh and tell him to let God's people go, Moses replied that he couldn't address the people like that because he was not eloquent, but was slow of speech and tongue (see Exod. 4:10). He basically told God, "I can't talk on Your behalf because I have a speech impediment." That didn't impress God. Exodus 4:14-16 says, "The anger of the LORD was kindled against Moses, and He said: 'Is not Aaron the Levite your brother? I know that he can speak well. And look, he is also coming out to meet you. When he sees you, he will be glad in his heart. Now you shall speak to him and put the words in his mouth. And I will be with your mouth and with his mouth, and I will teach you what you shall do. So he shall be your spokesman to the people. And he himself shall be as a mouth for you, and you shall be to him as God.'"

In simple terms, God was telling Moses, "You don't feel like speaking on my behalf to people. Fine. No problem. Then we'll do it this way: I'll speak to you, and you tell Aaron, and he will tell the Israelites what I have to say." So, each time Moses spoke to Pharaoh, for example, it was actually God speaking to Moses, who then relayed it to Aaron, who then told Pharaoh. They did it the same way when Moses addressed the entire nation of Israel publicly. God to Moses; Moses to Aaron; Aaron to the people.

It's somewhat similar when God speaks to you in church. For the most part, He speaks to you through your pastor. You may not receive it, but it speaks of God's order. When you are in church, God sounds somewhat like your pastor. When you gain the understanding that God speaks through your pastor (as we touched on in chapter 3), this will help you to avoid resisting that notion. Remember, the Lord told Moses that when he spoke, it would be as if God Himself were speaking. If the people rejected Moses, they would be rejecting God because Moses was not speaking his own words; he was speaking the words of almighty Jehovah.

Other examples of God speaking through human beings include when He spoke through Joshua, Isaiah, Samuel, Jeremiah,

Ezekiel, Amos and others in the Old Testament. God told the prophet Isaiah, in Isaiah 51:16, "I have put My words in your mouth," that Isaiah could speak on God's behalf to the people.

God said to the prophet Jeremiah in Jeremiah 1:9-10, "Behold, I have put My words in your mouth. See, I have this day set you over the nations and over the kingdoms, to root out and to pull down, to destroy and to throw down, to build and to plant." When Jeremiah spoke to the nation, it was God speaking.

In 2 Samuel 12:7 when the prophet Nathan confronted David, saying, "You are the man!" who committed the sin with Bathsheba, it was God calling David out through Nathan.

These examples display that when God speaks to us objectively, He most often does it through other people. We should be warned, however, that there are people who corrupt this principle. They may falsely claim that God speaks through them when He actually does not, or that God only speaks through them, when that, too, is false. The prophet Ezekiel declares judgment on such false prophets. He says they "prophesy out of their own heart" (Ezek. 13:2). Ezekiel goes on to say that God has not spoken to or through them. They are not speaking what God has said, but only what they themselves think. The Lord says about them, "I have not spoken" (Ezek. 13:7).

One of my college professors used to say, "Heresy always begins with truth and goes to an extreme." Heresy often has a kernel of truth in it. But it distorts that truth so that the very truth it claims to represent is neutered. The warning bears repeating: There are those people who will try to convince others that in order for you to get a word from God, you've got to go to a certain priest or pastor or preacher or prophet—to that person and no one else to get a word from God. But God is not so limited. He does not have to wait until you get to Reverend so-and-so, Prophet so-and-so, or Bishop so-and-so in order to get His message to you.

Prophets do miss it sometimes. I will never forget what a prophet of God once told me. I was out of town, preaching. In those days, other than the couple of hundred dollars I would receive from being a musician at a local church, the only income I had was what I made when I preached; this occasion was such a trip. My wife and I hadn't been married for very long. I hated being away from home so often, but I saw it as God making provision for us. On more than one occasion, my wife and I spoke of how much we missed each other. I shared with the preacher who was hosting me about how my wife expressed her loneliness. I told him I felt bad about being gone so much. And, as a relatively new husband, I not only shared the anxiety of being apart, but for me, my loneliness was accompanied by some guilt.

In the past, I had witnessed the prophetic gift in operation with my host friend. I had seen him make prophetic declarations that were proven true by the testimonies of the people involved. I had seen him prophesy about women becoming pregnant after extended times of frustration over their lack of ability to conceive; and they indeed conceived. I had not seen this brother miss it.

On this occasion, he approached me and said, "I've got a word for you."

"Yes?" I replied.

"Yes. Your wife is lonely," he told me.

"I know she is," I responded.

"I've got a word," he repeated. "What she *really* wants is a baby."

"Do tell," I replied.

He went on to prophesy that, "In six months she's going to be with child."

Exactly six months later . . . she was nowhere near "with child." The man had specifically said "six months." What he did not know when he implied "thus saith the Lord" was that my wife had undergone a very serious operation (in which she could have lost her life) that had left us incapable of conceiving. That prophet really missed it.

Dr. B. J. Willhite, a great man of prayer, taught me about the operation of the gift of tongues and gave me the most balanced theological and practical insights into this spiritual phenomenon that I have ever heard. Dr. Willhite is also a great man of wisdom. He shared with me how he had once heard a prophet give a word. Dr. Willhite happened to know the back story of the people involved, and he knew that the "word" could not be true. In his inimitable Arkansas drawl, Dr. Willhite said to me, "Brother Ken, that brother missed God." Then he added, "But don't worry. All of us miss God sooner or later!"

The truth is that sometimes prophets miss it. Sometimes they speak, and they haven't actually heard the voice of God. The point is that you cannot rely exclusively on waiting to hear from somebody else in order to know what God has for you. My congregation cannot be completely spiritually dependent upon me to hear every single word God wants to speak to each and every one of them. You never know for sure the many ways God will try to get a word to you, so we can't limit Him to one or two sources. (This includes those who call their church to see if the pastor is going to be preaching next Sunday so they can decide whether to go because God's truth is God's truth regardless of the vessel that truth is delivered through.)

Remember, the enemy wants to keep us spiritually immature by making us think that we can only get a word from one particular vessel. But when God wants you to know something, He will speak to you. Again, this does not negate your pastor's function in your life. Nor does it negate horizontal relationships in your life, including trusted and proven people in your life who walk closely with the Lord. It only means that God wants to develop a vertical relationship between you and Him. And part of that relationship includes and requires communication. If you never learn to communicate, you will never grow to be the spiritually mature woman or man that He wants you to be.

Subjectively

The second way God most often speaks to us is subjectively. This means that He speaks directly to our spirit, as He did in Acts 8:29 with Philip, prior to his encounter with the eunuch of Candace, queen of the Ethiopians.

This is not something spooky or weird. This is simply part of the normal Christian life, which calls for us to be in a relationship with God where we are in ongoing dialogue with Him. Many of us do not understand prayer because for most of us, prayer is a monologue (at best!). In too many cases, it's even a speech, where we bow down and have a diatribe with God. "Oh thou God of Abraham, Isaac and Jacob. Who was and is and who is to come. Magnificent and glorious . . . Alpha and Omega . . ." blah-blah-blah. Sometimes I don't have that much time to get all that out. There are emergency prayer times when I just don't have time to be fancy and high and mighty in word and speech— I need a word, and from where I sit, I need it right now!

God speaking directly into our spirit isn't something to fear. This is not God taking you into some strange trance. You don't have to have a special look on your face to hear from God. It's not that deep. We've all heard weird stories involving God speaking to people; such tales are supposedly "the model" for how and when and to whom He speaks. Don't buy into that. Some people talk "holy talk" and use religious jargon, buzz words and catch phrases. But it doesn't take all that to talk to or hear from God.

God simply *speaks into your spirit*. What does that mean? Now we can go a little deep: When God speaks to your spirit, He deposits thoughts, impressions and ideas into your being, your spirit, your mind, that are His will for your life. These things will *never* contradict His word in the Bible for they are God's Spirit giving revelation and insight into your spirit.

Proverbs 20:27 says that the spirit of a man is the lamp of God, searching all the inner depths of our heart. God speaks to us by lighting the candle of our spirit to reveal His will to us. Your spirit (not to be confused with the Holy Spirit), the spirit of a man, the spirit of a woman, your inner being—that is the candle of God. For example, Psalm 37:4 says that if you delight yourself in the Lord, He will give you the desires of your heart. It does not mean that God fulfills everything you ask for. It means that God deposits into your heart the desires that He desires you to desire. God lights the candle of your spirit to reveal His will. He lights the candle of your heart to bring thoughts, ideas and impressions into your mind, causing you to think things that are His will for you.

Whenever I used to say or do something that was really off the beaten path, my momma used to ask me, "Son, where'd you get that from?" When she was really mad she would say, "You didn't get that from me. Somebody's been talking to you, and whatever they said to you, you took it in." Momma knew that things that are spoken into our very being can often shape and form our thoughts and ideas. It's the same principle with God. If we spend enough time in His presence, hearing His voice, talking with Him, He deposits thoughts and ideas into our spirit that are *His*.

This raises an interesting issue. In Isaiah 55 there is a verse that has puzzled me. I've preached it. I've quoted it. I've taught it. I've shared it. And now I realize that it has hindered me and stunted me. God says in Isaiah 55:8, "My thoughts are not your thoughts . . ."—*whoa* . . . hold on. Doesn't He say that He puts His thoughts into our mind? Why then does He say in Isaiah 55:8 that His thoughts are not our thoughts? The revelation of the text is this: The thoughts that you think are your own thoughts are not God's thoughts. However, if you learn *to think the same thoughts God thinks*, then your thoughts become His thoughts. In other words, my thoughts generated from me in their carnality (thoughts that grow out of my own fleshly nature and mindset) can never reach God. So God says, "If you want to know about how much difference there is between My thoughts and your thoughts, go outside and look up. As far up as the heavens are above the earth, that's about how much difference there is between My thoughts and your thoughts." If we don't try to think beyond our earthly, human thoughts and strive to reach up to the mind of God, then we will never grow.

First Corinthians 2:9 is another verse that had me stunted. I quoted it. I preached it. I shared it, taught it, shouted on it, jumped on it. But I now realize that it had me in bondage too because I didn't fully understand it: "Eye has not seen, nor ear heard, nor have entered into the heart of man the things which God has prepared for those who love Him." We can't even imagine in our little heart and mind the things that God has for us. It is true that eyes have not seen and ears have not heard nor has entered into the hearts of men the things that God has prepared for those who love Him—that is all true, praise the Lord, *but* . . . then comes the next verse—and it starts with a "but"[2]: "But God has revealed them to us through His Spirit. For the Spirit searches all things, yes, the deep things of God" (1 Cor. 2:10).

Here's what the 1 Corinthians 2:9-10 text is saying: Eyes have not seen (by themselves), ears have not heard (by themselves), nor has entered into the heart of men (by itself) the things that God has prepared—but God Himself reveals them. In other words, we don't see it by ourselves, we don't think of it on our own, we don't hear it ourselves, but *only the Spirit of the living God reveals it to us.* Once God reveals it to us, then we've got it. Thus, it's not that we cannot know it; it is that we can only know it *if He reveals it.* Wow. I had always stopped at the idea that I can never know what God thinks; I can never know His mind; I can never know His ideas and thoughts. Because that's what the verse said. But I closed the Bible too quickly after reading Isaiah 55:8 ("My thoughts are not your thoughts"). And the truth is, I cannot know *in and of myself,* I can only know when He reveals it to me.

First Corinthians 2:16 perfectly illustrates this point. It says, for "who has known the mind of the LORD that he may instruct Him?" This is a rhetorical question, based on the verse that precedes it. It means that no one can have the mind of God until God gives it. But even this question is followed by another "but": "But we have the mind of Christ." *The Living Bible* translation puts it this way: "But, strange as it seems, we Christians actually do have within us a portion of the very thoughts and mind of Christ"—*bam!*—there it is. His thoughts are not my thoughts. My thoughts are not His thoughts. True. No argument. Eyes have not seen, ears have not heard. Yes, true again. *But* God reveals it through His Spirit. And His Spirit speaks to my spirit.

First Corinthians 2:9-12 teaches that God's Spirit speaks to our spirit. We have within us a portion of the very thoughts and mind of Christ. When we talk with God and listen to Him long enough, He puts His thoughts into our mind. His Spirit speaks to our spirit, and He gives us "the mind of Christ." You can't do this all by yourself; the Spirit reveals it. And when the Spirit reveals it, God's Spirit speaks to your spirit, and He gives you the mind of Christ, the very thoughts of Jesus. That's where God wants us. *He wants us to know how to recognize His thoughts.* If you think His thoughts, then you'll speak His words. If you speak His words, then *you know His voice.*

His Still, Small Voice

Exactly how does God speak to our heart? First Kings 19:9 begins the story of the great prophet Elijah. Elijah was depressed, confused and discouraged because things had not gone the way he thought they should. So he went and hid out in a cave where the word of God came to him: "What are you doing here, Elijah?"

This was a rhetorical question, to which Elijah responded in verses 10-13 with a recounting of his thoughts and God's replies:

> "I have been very zealous for the LORD God of hosts; for the children of Israel have forsaken Your covenant, torn down Your altars, and killed Your prophets with the sword. I alone am left; and they seek to take my life." Then He said, "Go out, and stand on the mountain before the LORD." And behold, the LORD passed by, and a great and strong wind tore into the mountains and broke the rocks in pieces before the LORD, but the LORD was not in the wind; and after the wind an earthquake, but the LORD was not in the earthquake; and after the earthquake a fire, but the LORD was not in the fire; and after the fire a still small voice. So it was, when Elijah heard it, that he wrapped his face in his mantle and went out and stood in the entrance of the cave. Suddenly a voice came to him, and said, "What are you doing here, Elijah?"

In this recounting, Elijah basically said to the Lord, "You told me to go out here and preach and I've done it; but no one is listening to me. And then when I did what You told me to do, they tried to kill me. You want to know what I am doing? I'm running for my life, Lord!" Then a great and powerful wind tore the mountains apart and shattered the rocks before the Lord.

But the Lord was not in the wind. After the wind, there was an earthquake. But the Lord was not in the earthquake. After the earthquake came a fire. But the Lord was not in the fire. But after the fire . . . came a gentle whisper. And it was in a gentle whisper, a still, small voice, where God spoke to the mighty prophet.

Notice that God didn't shout or yell or try to get above the other noises. Some people's lives are just too noisy. Too much clutter. Too much din. Too much busyness. Too much distraction. God is not going to shout over the racket of our lives. He won't even try to compete with the chaos. He is going to speak in the still, small voice. This means that our job is to get to a place where we tune out all the other stuff, and calm and settle ourselves long enough to hear what God is trying to tell us.

Hearing God is not a naturally occurring ability. It is something that must be learned. That learning process begins with our focusing on Him and getting to a place where the chaotic cacophony of life is not a competing distraction that pulls us away from seeking Him. The psalmist said it like this: "Be still, and know that I am God" (Ps. 46:10). My momma used to tell me, "Boy, you need to go sit down somewhere. You need to just go sit down somewhere."

We cannot hear God's still, gentle voice until we get to a still, calm place and say, "Speak to me, Lord."

Notes

1. Dallas Willard, *Hearing God: Developing a Conversational Relationship with God* (Downers Grove, IL: IVP Books), pp. 86-87.
2. Every "but" follows a statement; what was said on one side of the "but" is about to be challenged and adjusted by what is about to be said on the other side of it.

7

To Seek God's Word

Deuteronomy 17:15-20 tells about when God decided to grant the demand of the Israelites for a king to be set over them. He tells them He will choose a king from among the people, and will set that king as leader over the nation. Then God gives His qualifications for the king: The king must not trust in horses, not trust in his army, not trust in making political alliances through marriages and not rely upon his wealth. In other words, the king is to rule according to God's will, putting his total trust in the Lord and doing as He says. Then, in verses 18 and 19, God adds an interesting additional instruction for the king He is going to appoint over the Israelites:

> Also it shall be, when he sits on the throne of his kingdom, that he shall write for himself a copy of this law in a book, from the one before the priests, the Levites. And it shall be with him, and he shall read it all the days of his life, that he may learn to fear the LORD his God and be careful to observe all the words of this law and these statutes, that his heart may not be lifted above his brethren, that he may not turn aside from the commandment to the right hand or to the left, and that he may prolong his days in his kingdom, he and his children in the midst of Israel (Deut. 17:18-20).

This is an astounding instruction for the king. God wants him to *write out a complete copy of God's laws!* The king is told that he must write something in a book, something that he is going to be able to refer to for the rest of his life so that he will not stray from God's path and not become proud or arrogant, thus prolong his days as king.

I cannot emphasize enough the importance of learning to hear God for yourself. First Peter 2:9 says that we are royalty, a royal priesthood, a chosen people. In order to function in our royal call, we must learn to write down what God says, for He speaks to us through His Word, the Bible.

Many preachers have written daily devotional books in which they take a different Bible verse every day and write a brief commentary about it, thoughts to reflect on, to be encouraged by or to consider for that particular day. Max Lucado has a plan; Charles Swindoll has one. Charles Spurgeon wrote several, such as *My Utmost for His Highest*, *Spurgeon's Devotions* and *Streams in a Desert*. These are all very good devotional plans, but they are not *the* Bible. In other words, if you want to read, to study and to know what God says, you need to read *His Word*, not someone's word about the Word. The Bible (not someone else's commentary or daily devotional, but the Bible itself) is where we find what God wants to say to us individually. Too many Christians—possibly *most* Christians—simply do not search God's Word on their own to see what He is saying. So how could they ever even begin to obey Him? Sometimes people tell me that they listen to my sermon messages during their devotional reading time. I appreciate that, but I want people to read *the* Word.

When you go to church on Sunday, you corporately wrestle with the Word, as to how God is speaking in your house of worship. But when you go as an individual to the Word, you go to see what God is saying to *you*. So when you go to the Word, go with the assumption and expectation that God is going to speak *to you*. This is what God instructed Israel's king to do. God said that one of the first requirements for the king of the Israelites would be that he shall write down what God has said. This is a revolutionary concept for Christians who go to church mostly to see what the pastor has to say about what God has to say. But we each need to learn to hear what He has to say to us *individually*. To do this faithfully, we need to approach it in a way that will help us become disciplined to hear God's voice each day.

The question, then, is not whether God is speaking; the question is, *Are we listening?* God will speak to you every day if you will listen. To keep track of what He is saying to you requires that you *write it down*, just as God instructed the king of Israel to do. I'm not saying that we must sit there, hour after hour, day after day, and copy down the entirety of God's law. But if we want to learn to hear God's voice daily, we must follow a plan that allows us the most efficient and prosperous use of what limited time our busy daily schedule might allow. In this chapter, I want to help you formulate a plan that allows you to seek God's voice every day.

A Plan for Seeking God's Voice Daily

In addition to your Bible and something to write with, you will need two things to write in: (1) a daily God journal, and (2) a miscellaneous notes pad.

Daily God Journal

When you go to God's Word, have something to write with so you can record what God speaks to you and what you say to Him, or whatever insight you receive. Don't merely jot down occasional notes in your regular diary or a day planner about how good God is. Keeping a daily diary is fine, but don't squeeze Jesus into your regular journal. Get another one that is to be a journal between you and God, wherein you write what He says to you and what you say to Him. This is not to be a "I had a bad day today" journal. There's nothing wrong with that type of journal (they can be very therapeutic), but this is going to be spiritual, a continuing conversation between you and God.

A Miscellaneous Notepad

You will also need a separate notepad because when you get into the Word, now and then your mind is simply going to stray. Either you will be distracted and forget something God is trying to tell you in the Word, or you will go to the Word and forget what you just remembered you have to take care of that is important. On your miscellaneous notepad you will jot things like:

- I need to pick up some milk today.
- I left something on my desk at work.
- I've got to prepare for my presentation tomorrow.
- I forgot to tell my husband something.

It's not that these "daily life-do notes" are bad because they come to you during your time of hearing from God; they are just legitimate things you need to take care of at some point to keep to your schedule and stay in your integrity in life. This is a way to handle those things that will come up while you are talking with God, hearing from God, communicating with God. When you finish hearing from God, you can then go back to those other notes.

So, in recap, in speaking with and hearing from God, first have four tools handy: your Bible, your pen or pencil, your daily God journal and your miscellaneous notes pad. And last, you need a structured plan for keeping track of what God speaks to you. As you go through the Old and New Testaments each year, this plan will give continuity to God's Word. You will learn how to read and how to move systematically through the Word of God. Now you are ready to sit with the Lord, to grow in Him, to learn from Him, to revere Him.

Let's look at a simple yet effective plan for spending time with the voice of God.

How to Seek God's Voice Daily

"Daily devotional." "Quiet time." I certainly was familiar with those terms (although I had few—very few—friends who had made this part of their daily lives). My spiritual brother Crawford Lorritts, my spiritual father Dr. Larry Titus, and my longtime friend and prayer partner Dr. Jack Hayford, all had successfully and consistently integrated this discipline into their lives. But in over 30 years of ministry and 50 years of being saved, I had never heard a message or a lesson taught on the value of the discipline of daily time set aside with God. In the summer of 2010, God used Dr. Wayne Cordeiro to change that and to make an invaluable deposit into my life and spirit.

I am dean of the Oxford Summer Session of The King's University. It was during our 2010 summer session at Wadham College, Oxford University, that my friend and co-lecturer Wayne Cordeiro taught me the value and techniques of spending quality daily time with God and in His Word. Since then, I have made it a priority to spend time with the Lord in His Word on a daily basis. What I share with you here is a summary and paraphrase of what I learned from Pastor Wayne. I highly recommend the more in-depth exposition and explanation of this approach, which you will find in *The Divine Mentor* by Wayne Cordeiro.

Psalm 19:9 says, "The fear of the Lord is clean, enduring forever." The word "fear" in that verse is the Hebrew word *yir'ah*, which means "reverence"; reverence for God is clean; it has a washing effect.[1] To revere Him is to keep your life clean. God's Word detoxifies your motives and your mind. It cleanses your walk. It detoxifies your Spirit. Ephesians 5:25-26 says, "Husbands, love your wives, just as Christ also loved the church and gave Himself for her, that He might sanctify and cleanse her with the washing of water by the word." The Word cleanses, and there's nothing that cleans better than SOAP, which leads us to a great acronym for studying the Word of God: S for Scripture; O for Observation; A for Application; P for Prayer.

So, when you come to the Lord to speak with Him and to hear His voice in your life, come with a Bible, a pen or pencil, a journal and a plan. And then approach God's Word, ready to be cleansed with Scripture, Observation, Application and Prayer.

Scripture

If you are reading an electronic Bible, you are going to have to figure out a way to translate, write or highlight what God is saying to you because you want to be able to *write your response* to His Word to you. Writing it is hearing it, eating it, consuming it. That is what experiencing God's Word is all about: hearing His voice proactively.

Your Scripture reading plan might be, for example, to read three chapters. In those three chapters, the Holy Spirit will zero you in on a verse or a few verses that center on a particular idea. It will be like a magnet to you—and that is your word for that day; God will speak to you through that Scripture. Write it down. For example, if you are reading through the book of John, chapter three, as you are reading, perhaps the verse that stands out to you is verse 16. So you write, "For God so loved the world that He gave His only begotten Son." Write the verse or idea that speaks to you.

You may be tempted to write down three, four, even a dozen ideas out of one Bible chapter. An important tip: Try to focus on the *one* thing that God is speaking to you. Trust me on this: Resist the temptation to write more than one, because you will not remember the other two or three ideas and they may not necessarily be God's word for you for that day. You have *one* word for that day. Write that word down; it is your word from God for that day. Yes, all of the Bible is inspired, but not all of it is necessarily always inspiring to you personally every single day.

All of your reading for that day may be two chapters of "begats"—"so and so begat so and so"—five solid pages of begats. So there will be times when a particular reading is not inspiring, but *keep on reading*. Somewhere in there is a word for you from God, something important He wants to say to you for that particular day. For example, in parts of 1 Chronicles it says "so-and-so was the son of so-and-so and the father of so-and-so was the son of so-and-so," and then right in the middle of that lengthy recitation of two or three chapters of all those son-ofs and father-ofs, suddenly the name "Jabez" appears! In chapter 4, verses 9-10, it says, "Jabez was more honorable than his brothers, and his mother called his name Jabez . . . And Jabez called on the God of Israel saying, 'Oh, that You would bless me indeed, and enlarge my territory, that Your hand would be with me, and that You would keep me from evil, that I may not cause pain!' So God granted him what he requested." Before that little golden nugget was a string of "son of," "father of," "son of," and on and on. Flipping through all those genealogies, I discovered that sometimes God hides gems in the genealogic recitation list. Don't rush through your reading too quickly! You might miss a blessing. Another example is in the New Testament when it talks about the bloodline of Jesus. It's the son of, the son of, the son of, the daughter of—*wait!*—there's a *daughter* thrown in there? The pattern has been broken. Maybe God's word to you in that case is that He is no respecter of gender. In Christ there is no male or female.

What I'm saying is that every reading may not be so exciting, just as not every sermon I deliver to my church every Sunday makes everyone shout with revelation. Sometimes the will
of God for that service is that we rejoice and jump and praise
the Lord; and other times, if we are in His perfect will, we are at
the altar on our faces, broken, weeping, repenting from what
God has shown in our lives and needs to be changed. My point
is this: Don't expect the same thing from your time hearing
from God every single day. The first thing to keep in mind is
that sometimes your reading will not be all that inspiring.

The second thing to remember is that you may not always
even understand the word you are reading as you sit to hear
God. On those days, it's okay because if you are on a yearly cycle, you will come back next year and see something totally different in that exact same verse. You will have grown in the Lord.
You will have learned more and more. Every time you read the
Word of God, He will show you something different. You write
down the part you do understand, and don't worry about the
part you don't understand. On some days, 90 percent of what
you read might not make any sense whatsoever. So what do you
write down? The 10 percent that makes sense. I had one of
those days not long ago. As I was reading Ezekiel 45, I thought,
What in the world is all this? I was reading a section about the offerings, and the offerings in detail, and make the altar so many
cubits high and so many cubits long, and I didn't even know
how a cubit related to me. It was going on and on about bulls
and offerings and shekels when suddenly in verse 20 it said, you
shall make an offering "on the seventh day of the month for
everyone who has sinned unintentionally or in ignorance. Thus
you shall make atonement . . ." And I said to myself, "*Whoa!
Whoa, whoa, wait a minute! Back up.*" In this whole section are
the details of the blueprint of how to build the altar and how
to build the temple and how to make sacrifices and so forth,

and then two lines pop in, saying to make an offering for those who *commit unintentional sins out of ignorance*. That was my word for that day, right there. Have you ever committed any dumb sins you never meant to commit? That's your verse.

Observation

Observation means that the verse that God has highlighted for you is given in a certain setting. The point of observation is to zoom out the lens and analyze what is being said. We want to begin our observation with the question, "What did God mean when He said this?" Observe what the passage is about. You need to know who the word was given to, what the circumstances were, what God said before and after it, to whom He said it, what was going on in the text, what it meant to whom it was said, and why God said it to them. All of this is *observation*. In other words, if God shows me John 3:16, "God so loved the world that He gave His only begotten Son," I write down that verse, but my observation is that Jesus was having an encounter with Nicodemus; so I write down the context of how Jesus came to Nicodemus, how Nicodemus responded to the word that Jesus gave him, etc. Don't write a sermon about the word God is speaking to you through His Word; do it in just a few sentences.

As an example of observation, of all the verses in the book of John, the verse that stood out for me was John 1:48. So I wrote this: "Nathanael said to Him, 'How do You know me?' Jesus answered and said to him, 'Before Philip called you, when you were under the fig tree, I saw you.'" Here is what I observed in that word: "Jesus is calling His disciples. His invitation is Follow Me. He calls Phillip first. Phillip 'found' Nathanael and brings him to Jesus."

Note that the word "found" is not in quotation marks in the Bible. I put the word in quotation marks because this is what

I was observing as I was writing down the text of the passage that spoke to me. The text does not say that Nathanael was lost, nor does the text say that he was walking away. All the text says is that they *found* him, which is why I wrote "found" in quotation marks. It doesn't say why they had to find Nathanael, but I know why Jesus had to find me. If I look around and God is not there, guess who moved? If He has promised never to leave me nor forsake me and I can't see Him, who moved? It sure wasn't God.

Don't look for a shortcut. The experience is the interchange and discipline of reading and receiving, hearing and receiving. Here is what I wrote and observed: "He is calling his disciples; his invitation is to 'Follow Me.' Jesus calls Phillip first; Phillip found Nathanael and brings him to Jesus. When he gets to Jesus, Jesus identifies him as the true Israelite and talks about his character. Jesus says, 'There is nothing false in him.' Nathanael asks, 'How do you know me?' Jesus saw him before he got there and Jesus knew his heart while he was still away from him."

That was my observation; that's what I wrote down. You may see something else if that verse was the one that stood out to you. Each person will have a different perspective on what the voice of God is saying to them through His Word. It's like a diamond: with every change or twist, you see a different facet of the cut; sometimes subtle, sometimes dramatic. At this point, you might say to yourself, "Okay . . . observation. So what? What does it mean to me? Why would God highlight that verse for me and not any of the rest of them in the whole chapter?" That is what we call *application*.

Application
Application is the single most significant part of this *hearing God's voice*-plan. This step is where many people get lost. Hearing God's Word has become comfortable for us. Many believers feel they have mastered hearing God's Word, but the enemy will

make us so callous to the Word that while we can hear it, it has little impact on our lives.

Application means that we answer this question after hearing God: *How do I adjust my life based on what God just said?* Write the Scripture. Write the observation. Then ask the question, "What does God want me to do as a result of what I just heard from His Word?" For instance, when God spoke the Ezekiel 45:20 verse to me about unintentional and ignorant sins, I wrote something in my journal along the lines of, *"Lord, I didn't even know that I could sin by accident."* I wrote it just like that. *"And now keep me sensitive and guard me from dumb sins I never meant to commit and I really didn't know I was committing."*

From the observation I made about John 1:48, I wrote, *"The Lord sees me when I'm lost."* I stopped there. I wrote that very slowly. *"He sees me when I am lost when I can't see Him, before I see some evidence of His presence. When I feel lost He sees me and calls me to Himself. He knows my heart even when I'm away from Him. He knows my heart and still calls me to Himself."* That's what He spoke to me; that's how I applied to myself the one verse in the reading that stood out to me.

You will see something different or slightly different in applying your verse or word or passage to you because you will see it through your own eyes, mind, heart and experience in life. In my life, I was seeing that God sees me when I'm lost, so I wrote, *"He knows my heart and still calls me to Himself."*

Another example of application for me was in James 1:25, where it says, "The man who looks intently into the perfect law that gives freedom, and continues to do this, not forgetting what he has heard, but doing it—he will be blessed in what he does" (*NIV*). The blessing is in the *doing* of what God says. He has already said, "Be doers of the word, and not hearers only" (Jas. 1:22). Most people go to church to hear. But the blessing is not in the hearing; the blessing is in the *doing*. He says, "The man who looks intently." The phrase "look intently" is the Greek word *parakupto*, which derives from the Greek word *kupto*, meaning "to stoop and bend to get a closer look."[2] In other words, the one who delves into, who enters into the Word of God, and receives the revelation of God so he will not forget it and will walk in it, because it is in the *doing* that he is blessed.

Sometimes, application of God's Word for you for the day is that He wants you to know a new dimension of His personality. For example, if you have never known God as Jehovah Nissi, He might reveal to you that He is the God who leads you into victory; He is your banner. What does He want you to believe? It might be a day that He wants you to believe that no matter how bad the situation you are in that day, He is going to bring you through. The application is that you are going to apply that word into your life and believe, truly know, that He will lead you through this trial. Or it might be the day that He emphasizes to you the call for holiness because God wants you to walk in holiness, righteousness and purity—that's the application.

To recap so far, first write the *Scripture* that stands out to you. Then write your *observation*; zoom the lens out. Here you consider the setting: What was being said at the time this word was given? What was going on in the context of the word? Why did the Lord point out this particular verse to you out of all the others? When the Lord showed me the verse about unintentional sin, I had honestly thought you couldn't sin unintentionally. Now I know it's in Scripture because I read something in His Word that I had never seen before. I've been saved for 50 years, been in the ministry 30-something years, and I had never seen that before, the offering for unintentional sins committed out of ignorance. I wrote the verse; I observed that it was given in the listing of the building details and the blueprint for the temple. It was declaring which areas of the temple were for the various offerings, including offerings for unintentional sins. That was my *observation* of the reading. My *application* of it was that I have actually committed some dumb sins, unintentional sins. I sinned against folk and didn't know I had sinned against them. I offended people and didn't know I had offended them.

I recall a couple of years ago when a woman came to me and apologized to me, saying, "I've been mad at you for two years, Bishop."

"For what?" I asked her.

"You remember," she insisted.

"No. I really don't remember," I told her.

She explained to me that it was because I had offended her. And an offense is an offense, whether you know it or not. If I step on your toe and I didn't mean to, there's still an offense. God says unintentional sin is still sin. So I wrote down the application to my life: *"Lord, I now realize I have done some dumb things, some dumb unintentional sins."* And my prayer was, *"Lord, keep me mindful of the ignorance of my sins."*

Once you have read the Word, observed what stood out to you and applied that voice of God personally to you, then you do the final step of the cleansing process of seeking the voice of God: you take it to the Lord in prayer.

Prayer

Your prayer is related to what God said and what He wants you to do. Your prayer might be something like, "Lord, thank You for showing me this." It might be, "Lord, help me *do* this." It might be, "Lord, give me power to handle this." For me, it was, "Lord, help me to be more aware so I can avoid committing unintentional sins unknowingly against others."

Under the *P* for prayer, write the prayer as though you are praying it. Don't write the Cliff Notes version. Don't shorthand it. This does not go on the Internet. It does not appear on your Facebook page. It's not 140 characters on Twitter. This is your private conversation with God; and since it is between you and God only, you can misspell words, you can split verbs, you can make up your own grammar. You are the only one seeing what you are writing. God will hear what you're saying to Him. The point is, *write the prayer*. This might seem very unspiritual to some people, but the Bible is full of prayers that somebody wrote.

In writing it down, you are doing several things at one time: You are learning how to be specific in your prayers (don't write a two- or three-page prayer), you are not trying to be a theologian, and you are not "preaching" to God. It is simple, such as, "Thank You, Father, for loving me to You. Thank You for loving me and coming for me when I stray and walk away from You. Thank You for seeing me when I can't see You. I love You, Lord. Amen."

That's it. You can then go into your day being reminded that He sees you. When something happens in that day that makes you feel lost or that throws you off course or when you can't see God around you, you can remember that you started the day with Him saying to you, "I see you. I've got your back. In fact, I see you when you can't even see Me." You are armed with that word from God for that day. You may not know what's waiting around the next corner for you that day, but the One who gave you that word knows—and He's got your back. Just keep remembering, listening and communicating with Him.

When you get to know God's voice, when you spend time in His presence, when you take time to hear Him, talk with Him, seek His Word and His voice in your life, you enable yourself to handle anything that life throws at you. Because His voice guides you.

Approach your study and prayer time as a "20/20 plan": 20 minutes to read and 20 minutes to write and respond. Some-

times it's helpful or even fun to do these devotions with someone else—a friend, husband or wife. When you do it with someone else, just add another 20 minutes: 20 to read, 20 to write,
and 10 minutes for each of you to share. The best time for you
to do this is whatever time works best for you. The best time
for me is in the morning. I get up in the morning early and do
my 20/20 time of meeting with God.

Don't stress too much if you miss a day or two. Have you
ever had such a busy day that you forgot to eat? Did you try to
make up for it the next day by eating what you would have
eaten the day before, so you could catch up? Of course not. You
went forward from where you left off. If you miss a day, sometimes the enemy will attack you with something like, "Look at
that! I knew you couldn't do it. You really don't have time for
this." That is a lie. If you miss one session hearing for the voice
of God, just come back to Him next time. It's not a competi-
tion or a marathon. It's the blessing and joy of spending time
hearing the Voice that will change your entire life.

Proverbs 2:6 says, "The LORD gives wisdom; from His mouth
come knowledge and understanding." Here is a thumbnail definition of wisdom: *Wisdom is the God-given skill for living life.* Wisdom is simply skill for living rightly. It is the skill that God gives
us to handle the realities of life, the grist of life. One of the ways
God releases wisdom is through what He *says*.

Notes
 1. James Strong, *Strong's Dictionary* (Nashville, TN: Thomas Nelson, 1996), Hebrew
    #3374.
 2. Ibid., Greek #3879 and Greek #2955.

8

How to Hear God in Your Choices

Genesis 24 tells the story about Abraham sending his chief servant to go and find an acceptable wife for his son Isaac. In the second verse, Abraham told the servant, "Please, put your hand under my thigh [a symbol of making an oath] and I will make you swear by the Lord, the God of heaven and the God of the earth, that you will not take a wife for my son from the daughters of the Canaanites, among whom I dwell; but you shall go to my country and to my family, and take a wife for my son Isaac" (vv. 2-4).

The servant responded to Abraham in verse 5: "Perhaps the woman will not be willing to follow me to this land. Must I take your son back to the land from which you came?" In other words, he was asking Abraham that if he were to find a woman but she wasn't willing to come, should he go and get Isaac and take him to her?

To this, Abraham replied, "Beware that you do not take my son back there. The Lord God of heaven, who took me from my father's house and from the land of my family, and who spoke to me and swore to me, saying, 'To your descendants I give this land,' He will send His angel before you, and you shall take a wife for my son from there . . . only do not take my son back there" (vv. 6-8).

This section of Genesis 24 is a setup to the fulfillment of the prophetic covenant God had made with Abraham beginning way back in Genesis 12 (and repeated in chapter 15 and other places) that God would bless Abraham and the entire nation through him. And now, through Abraham's son Isaac, God is finally about to reveal how this blessing of the nations will come about. It starts with Isaac taking a wife. To accomplish this crucial task, Abraham appoints his senior servant, giving him two guidelines:

1. The woman must not be a Canaanite; she must be of like faith to Isaac. The Canaanite clause was not a racial thing; it was about being of the same faith. It was spiritual. Canaanites worshiped idol gods. Abraham's people were those who knew Yahweh, the God of Abraham and Isaac.

2. The woman must be willing to go with the servant back to Isaac, rather than requesting that Isaac come to her.

These two stipulations were the only ones given by Abraham to the servant for the job of choosing a wife for Isaac. Abraham added that the Lord would send His angel with the servant to prosper his way; and then he sent the servant on about his business. The servant could choose any woman he wanted for Isaac, so long as those two requisites were met.

In life, God gives us the parameters, the guidelines, the "curbs on the road," and then He lets us make our own decisions within those parameters. He will not tell you to wear the blue dress instead of the red one, or buy the silver SUV instead of the black sports car, or eat eggs for breakfast instead of oatmeal. Abraham didn't tell his servant that all wife candidates must have green eyes. He didn't insist she had to be a certain weight. He never said the woman had to be rich or short or tall or average. He didn't even tell him that he must choose Rebekah. He gave the servant just two specific parameters: The servant must choose a wife for Isaac based on her being of like faith and not a Canaanite, and she must be willing to go to be with Isaac. That was it. Then Abraham sent the servant to perform his task.

Let's pick up the story from there: By Genesis 24:12, the servant has packed his bags, gotten his helpers and camels together, gathered all of the provisions he's going to take along with him, left Abraham and has traveled to the land where he would be seeking wife candidates. Once he is there, he stops at a well, where he prays, "Oh LORD God of my master Abraham, please give me success." Thus, we see that the servant had initiated his assignment with *planning* and *preparation*. Then he began his actual search with *prayer*. In verse 10, he got prepared. In verse 12, he prayed, asking God for success. And in verse 13, he is at the well where the daughters of the men of the local communities come to draw water. He plans and prepares. He prays. He departs and gets into position.

Let's look at each part of this very organized servant's approach at carrying out his task on behalf of his master, the patriarch of Israel.

Planning and Preparation

The servant either knew already or he did some research and discovered that the people at this certain well were not Canaanites. He then came up with a plan. He had learned that, according to the culture, these women got together at this particular place during a specific time period. He obviously also discovered or already knew that these particular women at this well were viable candidates to consider. He then put his plan into action in accordance with his preparation.

We must never assume that the Word of God or the revelation of the will of God eliminates planning and preparation on our part. I tell our church staff that we should prayerfully, carefully and strategically plan the focus, direction and vision of our

ministry. We should diligently plan—but all of our plans are to
be in pencil. In other words, we should make our plans, but we
should always allow for the alteration of those plans by the Lord.
For example, as I am writing this, I am in the process of editing
and re-editing the manuscript for this book. When I come to
the final draft, I will submit it to my publisher and they will
make the final edits. That is what we should do as we plan and
live our lives. We should prayerfully plan our journey through
life, and then lift up those plans to the Lord for His edits.

In his heart a man plans his course, but the LORD determines his steps.
PROVERBS 16:9, *NIV*

Position

Once the servant had left Abraham, traveled to this certain land
and stopped at a well, he said, "Here I stand by the well of water, and the daughters of the men of the city are coming out to
draw water" (Gen. 24:13). The servant had gone to the well
where he planned to start his search, and he positioned himself there.

What made the servant go to a well, and why to that particular one? Why didn't he go to the well at a different time? Why
didn't he go to the other well down the road? The text implies
that he chose this specific well and that he chose it at this specific time. If he were looking for something other than a
woman, he would not have stopped at the place where women
gather. He did not go to a frat house where only the guys hang
out because he was not looking for a man. He did not go to a
town square or a marketplace where many different people,
men, women and children, would be congregating, buying and
selling. He knew he had to go where the women gathered—he
had to be in the right position. Since his job was to choose a

lady, he got into position where the possibilities were highest to accomplish his mission. The Bible does not say that his going to the well was because God gave him a word about which well and what time. He was simply trying to make a wise and informed choice. He did so by planning and preparing, and then positioning himself into a place to make that wise choice, trusting God to give him success in making his decision.

Likewise, after God gives us His guidelines, He then allows us to make our own choices within those guidelines. If you never go to the right places, you cannot expect to find what you're looking for.

Pray

The servant's next step was to pray. In Genesis 24:10-12, the servant got prepared to start his search by praying to God to give him success on his mission to make a wise choice in a wife for his master's son Isaac. It is there at the well that he prayed, "LORD . . . give me success" (v. 12).

To sum up so far, we know that the servant learned or had known key things about the culture of the people at whose well he decided to initiate his search. He knew that this was a place where the women gathered. He knew that women would not be there in the middle of the day because they don't congregate in the middle of the day if they are righteous and holy women. None of this came as specific revelation from God. It came from heeding the basic guidelines given by his master, planning and preparing, getting into position to make a wise choice, praying about that decision and then observing what transpired during the course of his decision-making process.

What this story reveals by this point is simply that *God does not micromanage us.* One of the great misunderstandings many people make about hearing God is to think that He gives us a message a minute or that He micromanages the minutia of our decision-making. There is nothing in the text that says that God told Abraham's servant what town to look in or which well to go to. Many people miss their position because they're waiting on God to tell them where their precise position is or to show them exactly how to achieve something. God speaks to us and guides us out of relationship with us. He does not give minute-by-minute details and instructions. He is not "always-on GPS." He gives us the guidelines and then allows us to operate within those guidelines as we see fit. You will seldom—if ever—hear God's voice give you lengthy, detailed instructions about what you should or should not do, or what you did wrong and how you could have done better.

The servant probably did not pray about which robe or sandals to wear that morning. I doubt if he prayed, "Lord, do You want me to take the brown camel or the black donkey?" News flash: God really doesn't care too much about what you drive to work. If you spent all morning preparing and praying, and then fasting all night and sending up burnt offerings, just to know if you should go to that party after the reception, you should have just gone to bed because the Lord neither slumbers nor sleeps and He doesn't need you staying up all night figuring out what you are going to do tomorrow night. God does not move that way. If you cannot make your own general decisions without a revelation from God, you might be suffering from spiritual immaturity. In the same way that we teach our children to dress, there ought to be a point where we let them get dressed by themselves. It's all part of the maturing process. God trusts us to make decisions on our own.

Going to the right well at the right time is not a deep decision, but it speaks of an understanding of the culture of the times, the things that God had exposed Abraham's servant to, the things he had learned and the wisdom he had gained. If Abraham trusted the man enough to go find a wife for his own son, then Abraham had obviously observed in his chief servant a proven ability to handle some pretty important tasks. The chief servant knew that particular well was where the good women gathered. If he were to go someplace else, the people might be the wrong crowd for the task. It is important that we be careful not to have a relationship with God where we expect Him to micromanage our decisions. He does not speak with us that way. God utilizes surprising economy with His words. He wants us to learn to hear Him and to heed Him, so He can send us on any task and be assured that it will be well done.

Your Final Decision Is in Your Details

Now let it be that the young woman to whom I say,
"Please let down your pitcher that I may drink," and she says,
"Drink, and I will also give your camels a drink"– let her be the one
You have appointed for Your servant Isaac. And by this I will know
that You have shown kindness to my master.
GENESIS 24:14

Once the servant determined that the women at the well were viable candidates as wives, he could then use his own sub-criteria to make a final decision. In the verse above, the servant is saying, in effect, "Lord, let's do it this way: The woman I meet, when I ask her for a pitcher of water, if she gives me the water and then offers water for my camels too, then she's the one." One of the tests for him was the water. That was his own parameter, his personal requirement.

However, even if the woman brought water for him and for the camel but was a Canaanite, she wouldn't qualify because although she would have met his criteria, she would not have met God's criteria. The servant would then face a decision: subordinate God's criteria to his, or subordinate his criteria to God's.

The second thing was that the woman must go back with the servant to be with Isaac. When Abraham instructed the servant that the woman must be willing to go with him, it meant that she should be available. If she has met the like-faith criteria and even brought water for him, his camels and the whole town, but was not willing to go back with the servant to be with Isaac, then she is otherwise occupied. In other words, "If she's not willing to come back here with you, then don't come and get my boy and take him to her. She's got to be available to come to him." It wouldn't matter how beautiful she was, how sweet she was, how humble she was, how funny she was, or anything else. If she was not available, then she did not meet the criteria, which meant she was not the one, which meant the servant needed to move on to the next candidate.

In making any major decision in life, our criteria for the choice is always subordinate to God's rules for the choice. God has an *option* to honor our parameters, but He has an *obligation* to honor His word. Likewise, we have the option to choose certain details, but we must *always* choose God's parameters.

Not every single thing God desires and wills for your life will necessarily be involved in the word He gives you for your destiny. All God had told Abraham was, "I'm going to bless you and I'm going to bless the nations through you" (see Gen. 12:2). He never gave any details about exactly how He was going to do this. If you're sitting around waiting on God to give you every detail, you are going to miss Him. Some of us are facing choices and decisions right now in our lives. Some people want God to give them detailed instructions for them in the word He speaks. But He does not operate that way. For instance, a young Christian woman might want to marry a man who is "tall, tan and terrific." Fine. Praise the Lord. Nothing wrong with that. Short, pale and hairy, whatever your thing is, that's okay—as long as the qualities you desire first come under subjection to God's will and requirements.

God speaks in principles, not incidentals. For example, 2 Corinthians 6:14-15 says, "Do not be unequally yoked together with unbelievers. For what fellowship has righteousness with lawlessness? And what communion has light with darkness? And what accord has Christ with Belial? Or what part has a believer with an unbeliever?" Abraham told his servant that the winning candidate for Isaac's wife must be of like faith. This means that, according to God's guidelines, a man can just as well choose a God-loving woman who eats meat as he can choose a woman who is a vegetarian, so long as they each express and confess love for God.

Several years ago I was watching a Christian program, the original *Praise the Lord* show, hosted by Jim and Tammi Baker. The guest that day was a woman who told her testimony of how the Lord brought her and her husband together. She emphasized praying specifically for her "perfect" man. She said she had prayed for a handsome man. She had even told the Lord how tall she wanted him to be, what kind of profession she wanted him to have, the kind of physique she wanted him to have, and included other very specific details in her petition to the Lord. She said she was letting her request be known to the Lord. She then told how the Lord surprised her. She said her husband was short, fat, bald and whatever his profession was; it was not what she had prayed for. I seem to remember that they were coming up on some significant wedding anniversary, 40 years or so. She testified about how surprised she was that she fell in love with this man who was so diametrically opposed to what she asked for and what she thought she wanted. The most important feature about this man was that he was a strong believer. It was not that she had blinded herself, gritted her teeth and dragged herself kicking and screaming to the altar with this man. Her point was that the Lord had given her abiding principles concerning His will for her life, and she realized that the details she had envisioned were much less important than God's principles.

God most often speaks in principles, not incidentals.

Living in the Will of God's Voice

Many Christians have an idea that God's voice and His will are like a pinpoint. But He's not so much about nailing a bull's-eye laser dot as He is about keeping us encompassed within His circle of parameters. Whichever dot we choose within His circle will be the one that honors God. The thing we have to be mindful of is not to go outside of the circle. God moves through providence, which means that He orders life according to His sovereign will; as long as we seek His will and follow His ways, then He honors our choices. There is plenty of freedom for expression, creative operation and making decisions in our own life within earshot of God's voice and inside the circle of His will. His aim is to protect His children from what exists outside that circle, where the world operates.

Living life in the will of God's voice (His laws) versus living according to the voices of the world can be visualized as the following, with the symbols representing our choices, activities, behavior and attitude:

THE WORLD'S VOICES
People living outside of the will of God's voice write their own rules, do their own thing, and open their spirit to the voices of the world (man's laws). They live life "all over the map."

GOD'S VOICE
God's children can do anything they want within "earshot of His voice" (His laws). They live in the circle of His protection.

When we operate inside the will of God's voice, we have the protection, the guidance and the blessings of Jesus, the good Shepherd. We have complete "free range" within the hearing of His voice (and the doing of His will), knowing that as long as we follow His guidelines, His commandments and His examples, His desires will become our desires. On the other hand, if we choose to live life outside the circle of the will of God's voice, then we leave ourselves open to the whims and ways of the world, with its onslaught of clashing, enticing and often destructive, confusing and contradictory voices and ways that don't necessarily serve our best interests—and more often than not, serve the interests of someone else.

When following God's voice, we won't always know the destiny of His path. God's criteria in choosing a wife for Isaac clearly allowed for more than one person to be eligible as the final woman. Yet, the woman the servant would choose would be the one whom God knew he would choose. Here's why: Abraham gave the servant instructions that were in keeping with God's will, and the servant was determined to follow Abraham's (and therefore God's) instructions first and foremost. This cleared the pathway to success. Thus, while the servant was on his way from Abraham to the well on that fateful day, God was ordering Rebekah's steps from her home to the well—even though the servant knew nothing about a young woman named Rebekah, and Rebekah knew nothing about a senior servant sent by Abraham to find her.

God's providential guiding is most often non-experiential. In other words, God is guiding us, and we won't always realize He is ordering our steps for a cause or destination that He will reveal in His own timing. You can probably look back at real rough patches in your life, very difficult times, extremely challenging situations, during which you wondered why on earth God would let these things happen to you. Yet you look at where you are now and realize that if you hadn't made those stops or gone through those narrow passages on your journey to your present place in life, you wouldn't be where or who you are today. God does this because He loves us and wants us to live productive and useful lives while including us in the unfolding of His plan for redemption.

The Voice of the Path

Abraham's servant prayed that God would prosper him. Several times in the text he used the word "prosper." The word "prosper" means that God would grant a successful journey. Much of our contemporary theology often defines prosperity in terms of material acquisition and/or financial gain. However, the biblical concept of prosperity is much broader than that. The New Testament idea of the word "prosper" used in the story of Abraham is the same word that is used in 3 John 1:2. It means "to travel a journey well; to journey well." It is a picture of the idea of success: to successfully travel a road or path. It is a compound word. The meaning of the root word places the emphasis on a road, a path, a street, a way. The prefix means "good" or "well." To prosper means this: God sets you on a path, and within that path, on that road, is God's will; and God navigates you on that road toward His destiny for your life. His voice represents the curbs on the road. His voice keeps you from veering off the path.

As the story of the journey of Abraham's servant progresses, he finally meets Rebekah. When they meet, she gives him water and also gives water to his camels. She has now met his criteria as well as God's. His mission, effectively, is accomplished. But he doesn't stop there. The servant wants to really nail down this decision. He doesn't want a mere "mission accomplished"; he wants a prosperous journey. Genesis 24:21

says, "And the man, wondering at her, remained silent so as to know whether the LORD had made his journey prosperous or not." The sign and the circumstances were in order, but he still waited because although she had met both his and God's requirements, he wanted even more information about this young woman.

So, in verse 23 Abraham's servant asks her, "Whose daughter are you?" He is now inquiring about her family life. He asks, "Do you have an extra room where I can stay the night? I've traveled a long way" (see v. 25). Now he wants to know what kind of personality she has. He wants to know something about her breeding, her mindset, her priorities, her family, her thinking. What kind of roots do you have? What kind of upbringing did you have? What kind of home training did you get? How were you raised and by what standards? What kind of person are you? Are you hospitable? Are you a welcoming, nice, kind person? Are you humble? Do you have the heart of a servant? He is about to make a crucial, life-impacting decision for the son of his master, the patriarch of the entire nation of Israel.

Although the signs looked good, for him the signs did not quite fully indicate that his search was over. It would be as if you were driving on the highway and you saw a sign that read, "New York: 120 miles." Just because the sign says "New York" does not mean that you have arrived in New York; and just because you are traveling 60 miles per hour, doesn't mean you'll be in New York in two hours. All that sign means is that you're on the right road. If you stop at the sign that says you still have 120 miles to go, you will miss New York by 120 miles; and if you don't take weather, traffic conditions, your fuel gauge and other variables into consideration, you'll be disappointed if you're not in the city in two hours. The sign is merely an indication of what's ahead, but not necessarily a guarantee that you'll get there when you think you should get there. Other considerations still need to be factored in.

It's easy to make a premature decision when we don't have enough information. We may not know quite enough about the person we think we want to marry. They may have all of the right external qualifications, but we won't know enough about their character, their nature, their priorities, their integrity, their values, until we inquire, watch and listen. A spouse is a major lifetime decision—probably the second-most important choice we will ever make. If we don't listen for, and heed, God's voice in this choice, lives could be ruined.

In the End, It's Up to You

The servant at last had all of the information he needed and wanted, but he still had to make a decision. All of the signs and circumstances were right. She fit every parameter that both God and the servant had laid out—and then some. In addition to all of that, Genesis 24:16 describes Rebekah as, "very beautiful to behold, a virgin; no man had known her." In the vernacular of today, she was "a keeper." Now it was time to choose. And he chose Rebekah.

We cannot remain in the paralysis of analysis indefinitely. Circumstances, the Word of God, and your inner spirit do not all necessarily make up the totality of God's will. They are indications of His will, yes, but you are the one who, in the end, has to make a choice. When the circumstances are right, God's Word applies to the situation and your inner spirit is at peace; still, at some point you have to make a final decision.

In Genesis 24:55, Rebekah's family asked Abraham's servant if he would let Rebekah stay with them for another ten days. Abraham's servant responded, "Do not detain me, now that the LORD has granted success to my journey. Send me on my way so I may go to my master" (v. 56, *NIV*). In other words, the job is done. Time to move on. God might be telling you today that it's time to make a decision in a matter that you have heard His voice about, but perhaps you've been waiting around, taking your time to decide, even though everything is in place. Now it's time to make your decision. Maybe you need a push. If that man is not ready to marry you, then move on. If that woman is not willing to come with you and be your wife, then don't beat around the bush. Move on.

When you hear the voice of God on a matter and His criteria are not met, then even if yours are met, you need to move on. On the other hand, if God's standards are met but yours are not, then it's up to you to make a decision. Sometimes you might want to be patient and wait to see if things change. Other times, you may have been patient long enough, and it might be better if you just move on. Either way, once you hear God on a matter, once His criteria have been satisfied, it's up to you to make a decision.

If you make decisions based on God's standards, your way will prosper. There is an interesting nuance in the biblical concept of prosperity. So many today want, expect and pray that God would grant them prosperity. However, true prosperity is a cooperative effort involving our participation with, and in, the very prosperity we seek from God. Prosperity is not something God gives us, as much as it is something into which He leads us.

Abraham told his servant, "The Lord, before whom I walk, will send His angel with you and prosper your way" (Gen. 24:40). There is a law of hermeneutics, a method or principle of interpretation, called "the law of first mention." It basically says that if you want to know what a word, concept or idea means, you would do well to discover how it was used the first time it appears in Scripture. In doing so, it will give you insight into the intent and the meaning of that word, concept or idea, and what it means when it is used subsequently. Genesis 24:40 is the first time the word "prosper" is used in Scripture. The word prosper not only means to "travel well" (as we have noted), but it also means to "push forward," to "move in the right direction." It's the idea of coming behind and giving a nudge toward the proper path on your journey.

His Sheep Know His Voice

Jesus picks up the idea of life as a multidimensional journey when He identifies Himself as the Good Shepherd, and the Way, the Truth and the Life (see John 10:11; 14:6). The term "Way, Truth and Life" could be stated like this: Jesus is the true way of life; He is the way to true life; He gives true life His way. He is the road, the highway, the street, the path to true eternal life. We are the sheep of His pasture (see Ps. 100:3). On this journey through life, the sheep need a shepherd who leads them. Not only that, but Jesus goes further to indicate how one can identify His sheep: He says *His sheep know His voice.* This truth is far more than a poetic reflection on the relationship between sheep and shepherds. It is a challenging criteria that reveals who is, and who is not, a true sheep of the Good Shepherd.

Jesus says that if they (we) are His sheep, then they (we) know His voice. They know it by its authority. They know it by its tenderness. They know it because they are familiar with it. They know it, and they obey it. Whoa! The validation of the sheep as belonging to the Good Shepherd is that they hear and obey His voice! I wonder if you are like me in that there are times when you don't act like His sheep. Once in a while there is something about my "sheepness" that contradicts my identification as belonging to Him. If He is my Shepherd and I am His sheep, then my life is to be lived in line with His voice. His voice of direction. His voice of instruction. His voice of correction. He is the Good Shepherd, and His sheep know His voice. In the weakness of my "sheepness," I often find myself listening to other voices. I wish He would talk louder. I can't hear Him. I can't distinguish His voice from the din of the world or the shouts of my own flesh. Or I am moving so fast (trotting through the green pastures that He leads me to) that I'm too busy being blessed to hear Him. And before I know it, I have drifted so far away that I couldn't even hear His voice if I wanted to.

I wrestle with the sheep in me. Don't come down too hard on me for saying that. Remember, "All we like sheep have gone astray" (Isa. 53:6). That's how we go astray—just like sheep. Sheep don't merely jump off the path. When they eat, they drop their heads and nibble, and nibble, and nibble. And before they know it they have gone astray by nibbling their way off the path—often, so far off the path that they cannot hear the gentle voice of the shepherd calling them back to the fold. More times than I can count, I have been that wandering, straying, nibbling sheep. All too often, my life has drifted so far that I can't hear the voice of the Shepherd.

What makes it worse is that the Shepherd doesn't yell at us. He speaks in a "still small voice" (1 Kings 19:12). Maybe the Shepherd is calling you now. Yes, right now—while you are reading this book. If you truly are His sheep, then you hear His voice calling you back to Him right now. In that hotel room. In that easy chair. Through that iPad, Nook or Kindle. You are His sheep, and He wants you to hear His voice now. He is not yelling. He is not fussing at you. He is not mad at you. He loves you so much that He laid down His life for you (see John 10:15). He loves you so much that He refuses to leave you wallowing there in your own lostness, off the path of His love. He is sending His voice, His word to you right now. All of us have strayed.

All of us have drifted away. All of us have sinned by turning
from His voice. And yet . . . He still calls us.

Softly and Tenderly Jesus is calling,
Calling for you and for me;
See, on the portals He's waiting and watching,
Watching for you and for me.
Come home, come home, Ye who are weary, come home;
Earnestly, tenderly, Jesus is calling;
Calling O sinner, come home.

WILL L. THOMPSON, "SOFTLY AND TENDERLY"

9

A Voice that Carries
You Through

*But now, thus says the LORD, who created you, O Jacob, and He
who formed you, O Israel: "Fear not, for I have redeemed you; I have
called you by your name; you are Mine. When you pass through the
waters, I will be with you; and through the rivers, they shall not
overflow you. When you walk through the fire, you shall not be
burned, nor shall the flame scorch you. For I am the LORD your God,
the Holy One of Israel, your Savior.*

ISAIAH 43:1-3

We all go through hard times in life. Nobody escapes challenges
and difficulty. When we receive bad news, the word that has
been planted within us prepares us to handle these situations
and carries us through them. This is why it is so important that
we learn to hold on through any bad news that comes into our
lives, knowing that God has not abandoned us and never will.

In John 13, Jesus gives the disciples some bad news: He will
be betrayed by one of them, Peter will deny Him three times and
He is going away from them. In John 14, however, He immediately follows up that bad news with good news: All will turn
out well, for He is going to prepare a place for them, He will
send the Holy Spirit to them and God will be glorified and His
plan will be fulfilled.

In John 14:26, Jesus comforts the disciples with this: "The Helper, the Holy Spirit, whom the Father will send in My name, He will teach you all things, and bring to your remembrance all things that I said to you." One of the ministries of the Holy Spirit is that He teaches us all things and then reminds us of the things He has taught us. As I touched on in chapter 1, God speaks by implanting impressions in our spirit, in our mind and in our thoughts. He impresses upon us truths and revelations. Then, at some future point when we need to remember what God has said, it is the ministry of the Holy Spirit to press the rewind button and recall to our mind what we've already learned about how God operates during our difficult times.

Many of the things you hear on a daily basis can tend to drift from your consciousness. Somewhere down the line, however, something will happen that will trigger you to remember that you've heard this word somewhere before. Many times, for example, you will go to church and whoever is speaking will say something and minister a word that, for the most part, does not apply to you right then. But somewhere down the line when a challenge crosses your path and you wonder, "How shall I proceed here?" something rises up in your spirit and you remember what God said way back when. Or perhaps you have gone to church service and afterward thought, "That was a nice service, but it really wasn't for me." And then somewhere down the line something happens to you and that word, promise or revelation that had no relevance to you when it was previously spoken, God now brings to your memory, and you realize that what He taught you back then applies now.

God's voice in the past is what carries you right up through today and into your future. There is no reason to fear anything you are going through for His voice is the same yesterday, today and tomorrow.

Fear Not

Fear not, for I have redeemed you; I have summoned you by name; you are mine. When you pass through the waters, I will be with you; and when you pass through the rivers, they will not sweep over you. When you walk through the fire, you will not be burned; the flames will not set you ablaze.

ISAIAH 43:1-2, *NIV,* EMPHASIS ADDED

I once had a professor who told his students not to skip over any words when we're studying Scripture because there is something in every word. In the verses above, God could have said "if" you pass through the waters. He could have said "just in case" you walk through the fire. But He didn't say that. He said "when," which means you *will* have to experience the waters, the rivers, the fire. That word "when" is not good news—let's just call it what it is. But He follows that up with good news: you'll go *through.* This indicates that you will come out the other side. And then He adds even more: "I will be with you; and through the rivers, they shall not overflow you. When you walk through the fire, you shall not be burned, nor shall the flame scorch you."

In these two verses, God speaks about what He has already done, and He talks about what He has yet to do. When He says we're going to go through something, He is referring to our changing circumstances, because "through" implies a process, a journey, moving from one place to another, progress, forward movement, change of scenery, a different perspective. In the midst of your changing circumstances exists the unchanging character and nature of God. God introduces Himself as, "I the Lord" (the Hebrew for which is the name *Yahweh* or *Jehovah*). The name is the same one God said to Moses in Exodus 3 when Moses asked, "Whom shall I say sent me?" And God replied, "Tell them I AM sent you." In the midst of our shifting situations, there is the unchanging "am-ness" of God. "I am that I

AM" indicates a continual Presence, His perpetual *now*-ness, His unchangeable nature in our changing circumstances.

God does not say, "When you pass through, I will be . . ." He says, "When you pass through . . . I am." By the time you get there, God will not be catching up. He will still be *AM*. There is a constancy in the character of God in the face of the change-ability of our circumstances, so that when we're busy going through something, He *is*. He is always *is*. In the past, He always *is*. In the future, He always *is*. This is a rock-solid assurance of the immutability of God always being there for us *no matter what*. His word is solid. His voice can be counted on every time, through everything. He does not adjust Himself to what we will need in the midst of our challenges in life; He already *is* what we will need. He says, "When you go, I am. Before you leave, I am. On your way there, I am. By the time you get there, I will not 'will be'—I *AM*."

It Will Happen

Let's just settle the bad news right now: You are going to go through it. I don't mean to be the bearer of bad news; I write this to you because I simply don't want you to be caught off-guard. You're going to have to go through various doors in life and not all of them will be comfortable to go through. There will be challenges, problems and attacks.

Some people don't think tough things are ever going to happen to them. The reason they think that is because they feel that they've been pretty faithful. They've been praying consis-tently. They've been going to church and celebrating His Holy Name. But even those of rock-solid faith must always be pre-pared for the blindside: You are going to get shaken and you are going to wonder, *What the—?? Now why did* that *happen to me?* And you are going to remind God how you praised Him and

how you worshiped Him and how you tithed and how you gave
and how you prayed and how you celebrated and how you were
faithful and how you helped the widows and orphans and remembered those in prison. Because in times of trouble, many of
us remind God how faithful we were, and we ask Him, "Why
me, Lord?" as if we did all the work for Him and now it's His
turn to do something for us. We go to God and demand, "What's
up with this, Lord? Why is this happening to me?"

To this, God answers, "Why not you?" There is nothing that
makes any of us so special that we shouldn't experience pres-
sures and challenges and hardship in life. The truth is, sometimes it's just our turn.

In 2008, when Hurricane Faye was headed for land, the governor of Florida declared a state of emergency to warn the people, "Get ready now!" When he declared the emergency, the sun
was shining, and the skies were clear. But out in the ocean, there
was a storm gathering, and it was headed their way. When an
emergency is declared, if the storm doesn't hit, you're still in
good shape. But if you don't prepare, when it does drop down
onto your path, you are in a world of trouble. The governor was
trying to warn the citizens that something was coming. He said,
"When this thing hits . . ."

Remember, God didn't say, "If you go through"; He said,
"When." But there's still some question as to *when* the "when" is
going to occur. The question of "if" means that it may happen or
it may not happen. But the question of "when" means *it is going
to happen*; we just don't know the precise moment it will occur,
which means it could happen sooner or it could happen later—
but it will take place. That's the bad news. Here's the good news:
"Whenever that is," God assures us, "I'll be with you"—and *that* is
the promise of His presence when it finally does happen.

Hear me today, child of God: You have the promise of God's
eternal word that you have His eternal presence. You are going

through. You are on this side, and you're going to the other side. When you go from this side to that side, God says, "I'll be with you." In between there and here is the "through." In Hebrews 13:5, God says, "I will never leave you nor forsake you." The word "leave" means "to send up or forth," "to release or loose."[1] God says in Isaiah, "I'll be with you when you go through" (see Isa. 43:2). That's a great picture. Here's the idea: to "leave you" means that *one projects forward while the other remains behind.* God says this, "I will never do that." He says, "Listen, you are going through. You're going from here to over there. But between here and there is the *through*—and I'm going with you during the *through*." I clung to that when my daughter died. I clung to that when my mother died. I'll cling to that till I die.

If God were going to leave us or let us deal with the storms of life without Him, His word would read like this: "You're going through. Now go ahead . . . go on over, go on through there. Bye-bye now." But that's not God's promise, because "to leave" means to have you remain behind while God goes on ahead without you. Instead, God says, "When you go through, I want you to know I won't leave you. I won't send you through without Me right there beside you." He is not going to let us go through it by ourselves. He is not going to get way off up in front of us. He is going to walk with us every step of the way, and whatsoever challenges and struggles we find in the meantime, we can handle in the name of Jesus, because *God is there.*

When God says in Deuteronomy 4:31 (as well as in Deuteronomy 31:6, Joshua 1:5, 1 Chronicles 28:20, and Hebrews 13:5) that He will never forsake you, the word "forsake" means "to renounce, without intent to recover or reclaim; to abandon." It means "to leave behind in any place or state."[2] It means "to quit entirely." But that's not the promise. The promise is that you're going through those choppy waters, and your God is not going to let you go through them all by yourself. Nor is

He going to get out in front of you. Nor is He going to lag behind you. He is going to walk shoulder to shoulder with you, side by side, every step of the way. It is essential that you get this into your spirit. You're going to go through it, child of God, but you have the word of God that He won't leave you and He won't forsake you—*ever*.

You Shall Not Go Down

To use another example from the old Charlton Heston movie *The Ten Commandments*, the greatest scene to me in that film was not when Moses parted the Red Sea. The greatest scene was a short little scene where the water had formed two walls, and the Israelites were walking through these water walls on dry land. You could see the water raging and roaring and storming on each side of them, yet the waters could not break through and gush over the people because the mighty hand of God was holding back the attack of the enemy, preventing the people from being overtaken by the deluge. Things were not quite as fortunate for Pharaoh and his Egyptian posse however: they drowned—for they had chosen not to heed the voice of God.

I learned to swim as a kid at Camp Ouatoga, a summer youth camp sponsored by the New Salem District Baptist Convention, near my hometown of East St. Louis (where I also qualified as a junior life guard), but there were two times in my life I nearly drowned. The first time was when I was in the Marine Corps, stationed at Camp Pendleton in California. I was body surfing—well, actually, *trying* to body surf. While trying to catch a wave, I was suddenly sucked under the water. I remember panicking, looking up, trying to get my bearings and realizing I was face down—I wasn't looking at the sky, I was looking at more and more water! I thought I was going to die until the wave threw me up on the shore and knocked the wind out of me.

The second time I almost drowned was many years after the failed body surfing attempt. I was a choir director at a youth convention in Fresno, California. Mattie, a girl in my choir, could not swim. One of the kids was playing around in the swimming pool and pushed Mattie into the water. I dived in, and as I was about to come up behind her (as I was taught), Mattie spun around in the water and frantically grabbed me around my neck. She was so afraid that she began squeezing me and choking me. I quickly realized that I could not breathe— I was going down, with Mattie hanging on my neck. There I was, trying to save her, and both of us were about to go under. My friend Darryl Bowes jumped in and saved both of us by prying Mattie's hands from my neck and pulling us to the edge of the pool. I learned an important lesson in that incident: *be careful who you reach out to save.* Some people will take you under, and both of you will perish. On the other hand, when I look back on that incident, I hear the voice of the Lord saying to me, "You shall not go down."

When my son Kendan was learning how to swim, they put some things on his arms called "floaties" and threw him in the water. I looked out in the water, and there was my little boy Kendan splashing around! I didn't know what floaties were—I thought he was about to go under. I yelled out, "Wait a minute! My son can't swim!"

Calm as a cucumber, the teacher said, "Don't worry, Pastor. He has floaties on."

I said, "But . . . what in the world is a floatie? Is he gonna be okay?"

"Just keep watching," she answered.

Kendan was splashing around, bobbing up and down, swaying back and forth in those floaties. And then he had the nerve—with his floaties on and still unable to swim—to wave to me! "Hi, Daddy! Hi, Daddy!" He still couldn't swim a lick, but the water could not take him under because he had something on him to hold up his arms and keep his head above water.

God says that you shall not drown, you shall not go down, you shall not be overcome. If you can just keep your arms up, if you can just stretch out your hands to heaven, then you shall go through the water. I am here to tell you, more hurricanes are on the way. Another Katrina is coming again. They always do. But they shall not overtake you. They shall not overflow you for you have the promise of the voice of God.

To the Glory of the Fourth Man

The third chapter of the book of Daniel tells the story of the three Hebrews—Shadrach, Meshach and Abed-Nego—who were tied up and thrown into the furnace because they would not bow down and obey the king. When the king's counselors assumed that all three men had been burned up, they opened the door and looked inside the furnace. Daniel 3:25-26 recounts that King Nebuchadnezzar's counselor said, "'I see four men loose, walking in the midst of the fire; and they are not hurt, and the form of the fourth is like the Son of God.' Then Nebuchadnezzar went near the mouth of the burning fiery furnace and spoke, saying, 'Shadrach, Meshach, and Abed-Nego, servants of the Most High God, come out, and come here.' Then Shadrach, Meshach, and Abed-Nego came from the midst of the fire." Amazing.

But something was wrong with that picture. They had put in three men. After the fire, they looked in and saw four men. "The Son of God" is the Christophany, a pre-incarnate revelation of Jesus the Christ, which means *God was in the fire with them.* The fourth man was Christ Himself. The counselor called the men out and out came only Shadrach, Meshach and Abed-Nego. There was a fourth man inside, but only three came out.

What happened to the fourth? Why didn't He come out?

There is no record that the fourth man ever came out of the furnace because Jesus knows that your turn will come. When the enemy tries to put you in the fire, Jesus will say, "Come right on in. I got you covered. I am here in the fire. You shall not be scorched. You shall not be consumed. You shall not be destroyed. You shall not be burned. And when you come out, God will get the glory. I'll stay in here and wait on you, My child, and what I've done for others, I'll also do for you." That's good news indeed.

Now for the bad news: You will have your trial by fire. Back to the good news: "Fear not, for I have redeemed you; I have called you by your name; you are Mine" (Isa. 43:1). Verse 7 of that same chapter of Isaiah adds that God created you for His glory. Ephesians 2:10 says that God created you as His workmanship, His masterpiece. The original word for "workmanship" is *poiema*, from which we get our word "poem." The creative process of writing poetry is to have the words fit in the right place, making sure that the rhythm of the lines flow as one (whether or not the words actually rhyme). God is saying that He created you and that He formed you. To *create* means that He is your source. To *form* means that He fashioned you. God created you on purpose, and He did so *for His glory*. His purpose for your existing is so that He might get glory.

The Lord brings you through the water, through the river and through the fire because He has a greater purpose for you on the other side: No matter what you face, God is going to get some glory. He created you. He made you. You are His. He says, "I have redeemed you." The word "redeem" means to "buy back," to "pay a ransom," to "bid and to buy off of the slave block." The apostle Paul says in 1 Corinthians 6:19-20, "Do you not know that your body is the temple of the Holy Spirit who is in you, whom you have from God, and you are not your own?

For you were bought at a price." It's a picture of someone who is incarcerated and, in order to get out, somebody has to pay the bail. God redeemed you. He paid the price for you. And you are His beloved and prized possession.

You may have heard the old story about the little boy who made a boat carved out of wood. Every day that little boy would come home from school and would labor in his daddy's woodshop to shape and craft and hone and outfit his little boat. It was his favorite toy, his prized possession. Each day after school he would play with that little boat that he had made with his very own hands. He would put a long cord on it and take it to a pond near his home and launch his little boat out on the water, and then pull it back in with string. Out into the water . . . back in . . . out and in.

Then one day the string came back with no boat attached to it. He began to panic. "Oh no!" he cried. "Somebody help me! Somebody please help me! My boat is gone!"

He ran home to get his mother, crying out, "Mother, Mother. My boat is gone!"

"Where is it?" his mother asked.

"I don't know," he said. "It was there. But now it's gone."

They ran back to the water and, sure enough, the boat was gone. The little boy missed his boat. He would come home every day after school with tears in his eyes. Then one day as he was walking home from school, he passed by a pawn shop, and there in the window was his boat. His eyes lit up! He went inside and began to tug on the owner's coat. "Mister, Mister," he said, "you got my boat! I made that boat! Give me back my boat!"

The man said, "I'm sorry, son. This boat was pawned and now belongs to me. If you're going to get this boat back, you'll have to pay for it."

The little boy went back home in tears. Then he got an idea. "I'll go and get a newspaper route!" he announced excitedly.

Every day after school he would go home, wrap papers and deliver them on his route. Wrap papers and throw papers, day in and day out. He really wanted that boat back. Finally the day came when he had a pocket full of money.

He ran down to the pawn shop, tugged on the coat of the pawn shop owner and said, "Mister, Mister, I got a paper route and for months I've been wrapping papers and throwing papers and finally I saved up enough money to get my boat back!" He began pulling money out of every pocket—pennies and nickels and quarters and dimes and dollars. He dumped it all on the countertop, and the man counted it.

"Son," the man said, "I think you have enough. You paid the price." He reached into the window, took out the boat and put it in the little boy's hands.

The little boy's face lit up. He said to his little boat, "Little boat, I missed you so much. There's no other boat like you. You are one of a kind. I made you. I missed you. And now I have you back. You are mine. In fact, you are mine twice: you are mine because I made you and you're mine because I paid for you."

God promises that He will be with you in the midst of your storms, because you are His. You belong to Him because He made you. You are not an accident. I don't care what circumstances brought you into this world, you are God's purpose. I don't care if you were conceived in a loving relationship or no relationship at all. You are His intentional being. It doesn't matter if you were born with a silver spoon in your mouth or you had to eat with your hands. God brought you here, and He made you so that He might get glory out of your life. No matter what you go through, God has got glory planned for you because you are His. He paid with His life for you on Calvary. Jesus hung between two thieves on a cross on a hill called Golgotha. Early on a Sunday morning He got up with all power in heaven and earth to claim and call His prize: *you!*

During the summer Olympic Games of 2008, Michael Phelps won eight gold medals, for a grand total of 14 Olympic medals to his name (the most decorated Olympic athlete in the modern games). Phelps said that the news and sportswriters in his hometown had claimed he'd never do it. They said the odds were stacked against him. People even suggested he withdraw from some of the events so that he might assure himself victory in the remaining ones. But Phelps knew that in order to even have a shot at attaining victory, he had to get in the pool.

Walk On!

As we learned in Isaiah 43:2, we are going through waters, through rivers and through fires. "Waters" is likened to the sea. When God says the Israelites shall "pass through the waters," they would automatically be reminded of the Exodus. God is telling them that when they come to the waters that look like they're about to overtake them, He gives them His word that the waters shall not overtake them, so keep walking on. I have two words of encouragement for you today, child of God: *walk on*. You shall not go down, you shall not be defeated, you shall not be overtaken. God is with you.

God also says in the same verse, "When you go through the rivers." If the waters reminded the Israelites of the Red Sea, then the rivers would have brought to their recollection the Jordan River. This is significant because the parting of the Jordan River appeared after the parting of the Red Sea. The nation came out of Egypt, walked down into the bed of the Red Sea and on across as if they were on dry land. They had now crossed over. Out in the distance were the hills of Canaan; they could see them. But now, between them and the promise of Canaan, was a river called the Jordan. "The river" represents those obstacles that crop up in life when we get close enough to see our blessing, but we're not quite there yet. This is when God goes into second gear. For example, in Joshua 3:15-17, as soon as the priests stepped into the Jordan River, the same God who parted the Red Sea parted the Jordan, whipping the gushing torrent into reverse and backing the water up "in a heap" on both sides. Then they stepped on across the river.

The lesson of the river is that when life throws you obstacles as you are about to flow into something new, some people will think you are crazy. But you're so close to your Promised Land, you can taste it. You've been dreaming about it. You've been thinking about it. It's been going through your mind. You aren't there yet, but you can already see it. You're starting to walk like you've got it before you're even there. It is then that God says, "Whatever river tries to stop you, it shall not take you down. You shall go through it. The waters will not overflow you." God says that you are going through, but in order to go through, you must first *step in*—but *through* means you will step out on the other side. You've got to get that into your spirit and your mind. You are going to come through.

So walk on, child of God. You shall not go down, you shall not be defeated, you shall not be overtaken, God is with you. So walk on. He brings you through the water, through the river and through the fire because He has a greater purpose for you on the other side: no matter what you face, God is going to get some glory. Whenever you experience tough times, the Spirit of the living God will press the rewind button, and His voice will remind you that you have His word to walk you through *anything*. He created you. He redeemed you. He paid the price and you are His. So, *walk on!*

Notes

   1. Spiros Zodhiates, ed., *The Complete Word Study Dictionary: New Testament* (AMG International, Inc., 1993); Gerhard Kittel and Gerhard Friedrich, eds., *Theological Dictionary of the New Testament* (Grand Rapids, MI: Wm. B. Eerdmans Publishing Co., 1985).
   2. Zodhiates, *The Complete Word Study Dictionary: New Testament.*

10

The Favor of God's Voice

I grew up in East St. Louis, Illinois. East St. Louis is a town about which they often ask (much like Nazareth), "Can any good thing come out of that town?" My mother lived at 1124 Tudor. On the corner near our block was a doughnut shop called (believe it or not) The Doughnut Shop that made bread and doughnuts. Starting at around 10 at night, we could smell the aroma of fresh bread and doughnuts being baked for the next day just a block away, and just after midnight, the store would open for business. My dad used to work swing shift at his job, and he'd get off work at 11 or midnight. On the weekends, the joy of our night was when Daddy would come home, and we'd get up and go down the block with him to the doughnut shop and get hot, fresh-baked doughnuts right out of the oven. Sometimes Momma would buy a little ice cream, and we would all have fresh doughnuts and ice cream in the middle of the night. The experience was out of this world to a little kid like me. It wouldn't have nourished me for long, but I could have lived off those fresh doughnuts and ice cream.

When Jesus said to the disciples in John 4:32, "I have food to eat of which you do not know," He was saying that He was sustained by nourishment not of this world. What was this "bread" He spoke of? What was He sustained by? In Jeremiah 15:16, the prophet Jeremiah identified this "spiritual nutrition" Jesus was referring to: "Your words were found, and I ate them." In other words, *God's Word* is what sustained Jesus above all else.

And it is God's word that sustains us, for man does not live by earthly bread alone. We feed off of every word that proceeds from the mouth of God. We are to be nourished by what He *says*. We are to consume His Word daily; we are to seek God's fresh voice daily. To understand that to hear God's voice is to consume His words represents one of the most significant transitions in your entire life.

In John 4:34, after Jesus told the disciples that He had food to eat that they knew not of, He explained to them, "My food is to do the will of Him who sent Me and to finish His work." Jesus was laying out the link from *hearing God's voice* to *doing what God says*, and how that simple yet powerful process equates to internal nourishment and the fulfillment of the purpose of one's life. Jesus was sustained by the "food" of *doing* what God told Him.

In Ezekiel 2:3-5, the prophet is being called by God to speak the word of God to the people of Israel. In preparing him to speak, God tells him, "Son of man, I am sending you to the children of Israel, to a rebellious nation that has rebelled against Me; they and their fathers have transgressed against Me to this very day. For they are impudent and stubborn children. I am sending you to them, and you shall say to them, 'Thus says the Lord GOD.' As for them, whether they hear or whether they refuse— for they are a rebellious house." In other words, God is telling Ezekiel that this is a rough crowd; they might not do as He says. But whether they receive God's word or whether they refuse it, he is to speak it to them and let the chips fall where they may.

There are times when God speaks such a challenging word that the people will shut their ears to what God has to say. There have been a few times when I have been compelled by the Lord to speak a word to my church congregation, and I knew before I even took the pulpit and opened my mouth that some of the people would receive the word and others would refuse it.

Throughout your life, God is going to say things that are going to be difficult for you to hear. You won't want to receive His word. You will want to shut out His voice entirely; it's so abrasive to your will. God said to Ezekiel right up front that he was to speak God's words to the people, and whether they received it or refused it, whether they liked it or didn't like it, whether they patted him on the back or stabbed him in the back, he was to *speak it.*

God continued instructing Ezekiel in verses 6-8, saying, "And you, son of man, do not be afraid of them nor be afraid of their words, though briers and thorns are with you and you dwell among scorpions; do not be afraid of their words or dismayed by their looks, though they are a rebellious house. You shall speak My words to them, whether they hear or whether they refuse, for they are rebellious. But you, son of man, hear what I say to you. Do not be rebellious like that rebellious house." I am embarrassingly challenged by this particular revelation because I am painfully reminded of times when I went into the pulpit with a word of God that I had studied and prepared that I might release it into the lives of the congregation. I meditated on it all week. I prayed and labored over it for days on end that I might feed the people the word of God and yet, I hadn't sufficiently sought His voice for my own self before attempting to take His Word to the people. Then come the next verses:

Now when I looked, there was a hand stretched out to me; and behold, a scroll of a book was in it. Then He spread it before me; and there was writing on the inside and on the outside, and written on it were lamentations and mourning and woe. Moreover He said to me, "Son of man, eat what you find; eat this scroll, and go, speak to the house of Israel." So I opened my mouth, and He caused me to eat that scroll. And He said to me, "Son of

man, feed your belly, and fill your stomach with this
scroll that I give you." So I ate, and it was in my mouth
like honey in sweetness (Ezek. 2:9–3:3).

Ezekiel takes God's word and, metaphorically, he eats it,
consumes it, takes it into his being. In other words, if you merely
cursorily examine what God says, you will never be nourished
by it. So where is the sweetness if the realities of life include some
bitterness? The sweetness comes in hearing God's voice and
heeding His words in the tough times. There is no "trial elimi-
nation" clause in our salvation contract. God does not exempt
us from struggles and challenges, but He does speak a word to
us to let us know that there is something on the other side of the
trial, on the other side of the pain, on the other side of the struggle. As we learned in the previous chapter, He will give you favor
to walk through it. Although you're struggling like everybody
else, God speaks a word in your spirit that tells you that you are
coming through this thing by the power of His Spirit, who
speaks a word to you that says, "Go on with favor in your life."

If you merely admire how attractive and beautiful the
words are and how poetic it all sounds, they will never nourish
you. God says to *consume it*. Because it is only after you ingest
and digest it that God's Word becomes part of your whole being. Then you can accurately speak out to others what God has
spoken into you. God's Word, His voice, is as nourishment to
our entire body, mind, spirit and being.

Man doth not live by bread only, but by every word that
proceedeth out of the mouth of the LORD doth man live
(Deut. 8:3, *KJV*).

How have you allowed God's Word to impact how you handle your money? Has the Word of God affected how you treat

those you love? Has what God says influenced how you behave around people? After hearing from God, has your attitude changed any? How are you in the patience department? There is something in the Word of God to deal with *every single area* of your life. How often do you absorb what God has to say to you?

Too many of us want the product without the process. We want favor all day long, favor on our businesses, favor on our lives, favor on our relationships. We want God's favor; yet we don't seek Him daily. God speaks *daily*. He says something to you *every day*. As you wait with Him to hear His Word daily, He will speak to you for that day. And because He speaks a word and you're hearing Him daily, you are now walking in favor because favor is an overflow of your relationship with God—a relationship that is nurtured *daily*. The person favored of God listens to Him daily, speaks daily with Him, has a desire to hear His voice on a daily basis. Even in the hard times when they can't seem to get a word, they come back daily because they know that when God speaks, sooner or later He releases favor.

The Voice from Behind

Isaiah 30:21 tells how God speaks to us daily: "Whether you turn to the right or to the left, your ears will hear a voice behind you, saying, 'This is the way; walk in it'" (*NIV*). There's a voice behind you that says, "This is the way." The voice speaks to us from behind. So, why is the voice *behind* us? If we are His sheep, and shepherds lead sheep (so the sheep are behind the shepherd), how can the sheep hear the voice of the shepherd behind them if he's in front, leading them? Here's how: We, like sheep, have gone astray. "Astray" means "have gone aside"; we have turned aside from God. When I turn aside from God, I'm no longer going in His way; I'm now going another way. When I go down another way, my back is turned to God. And as I go farther down my own way, I'm going farther away from God, which means that He who was in front of me is now behind me. But He loves me too much to watch me go down the wrong way, so He speaks to me from behind, saying, "Hey. Hey. Don't go down the wrong road. Hey. Turn left at the corner. Don't go the other way. There is a way that seems right to you, but the end of that way is destruction. I am *the* way, the truth, the life. Come back and follow Me. Turn from a way and go *My* way. If you go this way, you'll have victory."

When God is speaking into your ear, there's something about His Spirit that heightens your senses. When you are walking with God, He enhances your perception so you are able to hear things that no one else can hear. In Santa Monica, California, there is a very famous landmark called "The Stairs." My trainer, Natasha Kufa, introduced me to the famous cardio workout place. I remember one particular time going to The Stairs to exercise. I had my iPod on, I had a little rhythm going and folks behind me were probably wondering, *Why is he going so slow?* They didn't realize that I could hear something in my ear. They wanted me to go faster. No, no—I've got to stay on rhythm. They didn't know what I was listening to in my ear. It was Marvin Gaye singing, "Gotta Give It Up." Although I was rocking and stepping to the words of Marvin's classic song, it was as if the Lord was making a new "application" of that message for me and my life. As I jammed my way step by step to the top of The Stairs, the voice of the Lord seemed to drown out Marvin's and I could hear: "You've got to give this up, you've got to give that up, and come up to the top of the hill. I've got a blessing for you." My body was aching, but I had joy in my spirit because I was walking to the beat of a different drummer. I could hear God's Voice in the ear of my spirit.

God has you reading this book today to tell you that you can't listen to what everybody says to you because they can't hear what God is speaking to you. You can't run with everybody because they are not necessarily going where God's voice is telling *you* to go. God is speaking to *you* and His voice says, "Go in THE way." He may be speaking into your ear right now. You've got a revelation that not everybody can see. You've got a dream that not everybody can envision. You've got an idea spoken into your spirit by God's voice saying to you, "I will speak to you in your ear and not everybody can hear it; but listen to Me and walk in the way that I shall show you. It is the way of favor."

The Satan Psyche-Out

God says that there is a way that seems right, but the end of it is destruction (see Prov. 14:12; 16:25). When God says, "a way that seems right," the destruction inherent in "*a* way" is not necessarily apparent, it's not always obvious—which is why it *seems* right. If a sign says, "This is a bad way," most fools would go another way. But the devil knows that you aren't most fools, so he doesn't put a sign up to help make it clear this is a wrong way. But God has said in His Word that there is "a way" that leads to destruction, a broad, wide way that leads to death.

When God's voice speaks to you, saying, "Go in the way that I shall show you"—right then is when the devil will play his trick. If the timing of seeking God's way, His voice, His word, is not *daily*, then a way is open for the psyche-out of the enemy: Satan knows that God must be true to His Word, so he will direct you to a way that seems right to you and seems to have no negative consequences. The longer you go the *no consequences-*way, the more comfortable you become with going down that road. The psyche-out of the devil is that he leads you onto a path where judgment is delayed—but that's his setup because he knows the longer God delays judgment, the more you assume it can't be that bad. So, rather than repent and turn back to God's way, you say, "Well, I made it this far and nothing happened. Let's go a little farther. God probably didn't mean what was said way back in Bible days; that's probably a narrow interpretation of the Word of God"—and before you know it, you're comfortable with compromising the ways of God.

I am always amazed at how much I miss when I read the Word. At any given reading, I miss stuff or skip over things that I see later and wonder, "Hmmm . . . now how did I miss that?" I have read through Ecclesiastes, but Wayne Cordeiro is responsible for helping me look at Ecclesiastes 8:11 in a new light. This verse is a revelation of one of the devil's most common tricks against us.

The *King James Bible* says, "Because the sentence against an evil work is not executed speedily, therefore the heart of the sons of men is fully set in them to do evil."

The *New International Version* puts it this way: "When the sentence for a crime is not quickly carried out, the hearts of the people are filled with schemes to do wrong."

THE MESSAGE says this: "Because the sentence against evil deeds is so long in coming, people in general think they can get by with murder."

The *Living Bible* states it as: "Because God does not punish sinners instantly, people feel it is safe to do wrong."

In other words, it's a setup! The devil knows that God *will* be true to His word, so he gambles, and bets that, sure, God will pronounce judgment on you, but he places the odds at somewhere between judgment and mercy. Even the devil knows that it is the mercy of God that delays judgment. The devil puts his spin on "mercy" and uses that to try to convince us that God really doesn't mean what He says about consequences. Therefore, what at first bothered you about your sinning soon becomes comfortable because, after all, nothing has happened. God didn't seem bothered by your iniquity. Maybe all is well;

He didn't mind your not heeding His voice. You got away with ignoring His Word. So, since there were no consequences, instead of repenting for that sin yesterday when you prayed, you went ahead and did it again the next day. And again the day after that. And the following week. And what should have been an immediate *no!*—what might have been a one-night stand, a one-time rendezvous—is now a full-blown affair. And you think that since a hammer didn't drop on you . . . maybe it's not such a bad thing you're engaging in.

The devil wants to delay your repentance until the judgment has so piled up that what should have cost you repentance will now cost you your integrity, your marriage, your family, your job, your character, your reputation and maybe even your life. It's the devil's psyche-out because Satan plays on the truth that sooner or later God will get you. So the devil says, "The longer I can have you away from God, and His judgments pile up and the consequences pile up, the more I get the victory." With the devil's work, you get the consequences after the fact.

Ecclesiastes 8:11 should drive us down to our knees every time we sin because we should recognize that the longer God delays judgment, the worse off we will be when He declares "Enough!" A recent example might be the Tiger Woods affair. One woman after another after another. How many times did he hear a voice telling him somewhere in his conscience, "Don't go there, man! Don't do it! You've got too much to lose." If you're going to sin anyway, at least don't be even more foolish by doing it with people who don't have as much to lose as you do because the devil uses things like that—he knows judgment delayed will harden your heart; yet, you may be in a game with people who don't have nearly as much to lose as you do because even in the face of God they don't care what they engage in. But *you* better care! Disobeying God is one thing—He will judge you for that (He has to, it's how He teaches and grows us), but it's a whole other thing to completely, self-destructively, blatantly mess up your entire life with the sin you engage in.

When there has been favor on your life, it means God has invested in you. When there is favor on your life, it means He is granting you mercy and grace. When there's favor on your life, you've got too much to lose to suddenly start kicking at the goads and ignoring the voice of God. The devil does not come just to make you lose some of what you've got. He does not come only to embarrass you. He does not come to merely cripple you. He comes to *steal*, to *kill*, and to *destroy—everything*. And by the power of God, you've got to have enough sense, wisdom and plain old fear of God to say, "No! I'm trusting God to bring me through this mess. I need favor. I need the voice of God. I will not sin!"

The devil will trick you. He will set you up for a fall. That's how he rolls. As surely as you have, in your life, turned your back to God when faced with the enticement of temptation, God speaks a word behind you in your ear, saying, "Don't do it." Heed His voice while you can, for judgment delayed will harden your heart . . . and God will *always* balance His books.

11

Stuck, Waiting on a Word

What happens when God doesn't speak? What about those times when you can't hear His voice at all? Have you ever been waiting on a word from God and all you hear is . . . nothing? There's a story in the eleventh chapter of the gospel of John that tripped me up when I put myself in the position of the various characters in the story.

> Now a certain man was sick, Lazarus of Bethany, the town of Mary and her sister Martha. It was that Mary who anointed the Lord with fragrant oil and wiped His feet with her hair, whose brother Lazarus was sick. Therefore the sisters sent to Him, saying, "Lord, behold, he whom You love is sick" (John 11:1-3).

The story is picked up again in verse 17: "So when Jesus came, He found that he [Lazarus] had already been in the tomb four days."

There are two scenes in this story. In this scene, Mary and Martha are identified as the sisters of Lazarus. This is the same Mary who anointed the feet of Jesus, which means she had a relationship with Him. Lazarus was their brother. The Bible says that Lazarus is the one whom Jesus loved (see John 11:5). Thus, we know that Lazarus had a relationship with Jesus, too. That is the setup of the scene. In verse 3, the scene fades with Mary and

Martha sending for Jesus to come to them in Bethany because the one whom He loves is sick.

Word gets to Jesus that Mary and Martha urgently need Him to come to Bethany. It's life or death. His good, close friends in Bethany, less than two miles down the road, are calling out to Him. The average person walks three or four miles per hour. When the news reaches Jesus that Lazarus is sick, does He rush over to Bethany? No. He has a conversation with the disciples, telling them that Lazarus is sick but He has it under control. Then He casually tarries in Jerusalem. In fact, He has it so much under control that He hangs out in Jerusalem for *four days*, taking His own sweet time to mosey on over to Bethany, less than an hour's walk away.

Remember, Jesus has already declared in Jerusalem that He was going to handle the problem over in Bethany. But Mary and Martha were over there in Bethany, and they didn't hear what Jesus was saying over there in Jerusalem. So there they are, four days stuck, waiting on a word. Four days waiting for Him to come and fix a problem that He already declared He was going to fix.

Have you ever been stuck, waiting for a word and wondering when the word would show up? It can be nerve-wracking—especially if it's a dire emergency. If someone is dying in an emergency room, waiting for a doctor, they generally don't have to wait four days. Maybe four hours, but never four days. When Jesus finally arrived, Lazarus was dead. It was too late. He'd been in the grave for four days and had by then been reduced to a deteriorating corpse. That means that for four days there was the sound of silence from God, who was just a few miles away. It would be as if Jesus was on the other side of town and you were sick, on this side of town; and for four days you were waiting on Him to come heal you. And He's just across town. And you die—days before He even shows up.

The Bible says that these three people had a *relationship* with Jesus. Mary had anointed His feet while Martha had flitted about, tending to guests. Martha had probably cooked for him many times. They were, in fact, the family He frequently stayed with when He was in Bethany. Maybe their home was in a place of privacy, and they recognized that He could come there to rest and rejuvenate. They weren't just using their association with His name to try to get Him to go see them in a time of dire need for their brother Lazarus. Jesus was practically *family*.

Has anybody ever used your name to try to gain favor or influence with someone in a time of need? Have you ever had long-lost cousins show up after you got a little money or some property? That was not the case here. Mary, Martha and Lazarus had a close and genuine relationship with Jesus of Nazareth. It was out of that relationship that they had sent for Him. And for four days, He never appeared. A couple hours walk away. Never even sent word.

They probably wouldn't have minded at all if He had sent word back to them. Any excuse would have been fine, even something like, "Got your message. I'm coming. I'm a little tied up. Donkey threw a shoe. Camels are in a traffic jam at the corner of Jericho Road and Jerusalem Square. Traffic lights are out of whack. We can't get through here. But tell 'em I'm coming. I'll just be a little late." Because He was in relationship with them.

Or He could have done what he did in Matthew 8:6 when the centurion told Jesus, "Lord, my servant is lying at home paralyzed, dreadfully tormented." To which Jesus responded, "I will come and heal him" (v. 7). The centurion replied to the effect of, "Well, thank You. But I know You're a busy man. You don't have to come all the way to my house—in fact, I'm not even worthy of Your even being under my roof. I'll tell You what You can do, though: You are a man with authority and I know what authority is like because I'm a man in authority, too. I know that when You speak, things happen. So how about this: You don't have to change Your itinerary to come to my house. Just speak the word here and my servant will be healed over there" (see v. 9). And sure enough, even before the centurion got from there to home, his servant was healed.

Likewise, Jesus could have sent a messenger to Mary and Martha, saying, "Tell them I got it handled. I'm going to deal with Lazarus the same way I handled the centurion's servant. Just remind them that I am so much God that I already knew they needed Me to come; and I'm so much God that I can speak healing over here, and it will heal Lazarus over there. Go tell them that."

Jesus could have merely spoken a word—and *BAM!*—Lazarus would have been sitting at the supper table that same night. But He didn't. He didn't say a word. Instead, He chose to handle it in an unusual and very unexpected way. I'm sure He knew Mary and Martha were going to be disappointed that He didn't run on up to Bethany as soon as they got word to Him that Lazarus was dying. But Jesus knew Lazarus was dying. *That was part of His plan.* Because He had something in mind that was going to raise their faith to a whole new level. And the plan called for Lazarus to be good and dead, well before He arrived. I once heard my friend Bishop Charles Blake say, "God never shows up until He can get all the glory." Well, Jesus was making sure He got all the glory.

The Discipline of Disillusionment

In the meantime, however, Martha and Mary were stuck, waiting on a word and mired in disillusionment with their Lord and Master. Mary, Martha and Lazarus would have known about Jesus having healed the centurion's servant with a mere word. He could have done the same thing for Lazarus. But He chose not to do it that way this time. So for them, it was the sound of silence. It would've been better if He'd at least sent a late word; late is better than no word at all. They were stuck, waiting on a word.

You may know some Marys and Marthas in your life who are waiting for a word from God. You might even be dealing with the sound of silence from the Lord right now in your life. The text says that by the time Jesus got to Bethany, there were friends and people from the city who had gathered, which means now the situation had become public. Everybody knew they were trusting on Jesus to come and save Lazarus. You can imagine that first day after they got word to Him about Lazarus's condition that their friends and neighbors probably played it off:

"Well. You know. He's a busy Lord—everybody knows that. But He's coming. He's coming. It'll be all right; He's your friend, after all. He's surely coming."

Second day: "Yeah, well . . . He'll be here. I'm sure."

Third day, everybody would be getting a little nervous: "Anybody seen Him? You sure you sent the message to the right Lord? Go get that little boy down the street there and have him run down the road and see if he sees Jesus coming."

By Friday, they would be freaking out because by then it was four days of utter silence. By then, everyone in Bethany would have known. By then, gossiping tongues would have been clucking: "They *sure* they know that Rabbi? 'Cause He sure isn't showing up around here. Why would He do them that way?"

Not only were Mary and Martha probably very confused, but also they may have even felt publicly embarrassed. They had gone out on a limb and told everyone, "It's going to be alright. We sent for Jesus. Lazarus is sick right now, but it's alright. *Jesus* is coming!"

Has that ever happened to you? You're out on a limb. You've told all of your friends that something big is going to happen.

They're waiting expectantly on you to show them what you said Jesus was going to come and do for you because Jesus is your friend. And . . . nothing. We know how it feels, us churchgoers, us tithers, us prayers, us tongue talkers, us Bible readers: we are out there now and . . . no word. Nothing at all. It's just the sound of silence.

I've been there, done that, got the T-shirt and the hat. There have been times when I have gone public and shared with our congregation about a prayer request I had laid before the Lord. There have also been times when I was embarrassed and confused while waiting on a word or answer from the Lord that either seemed to be delayed, denied or ignored. I know how the sisters felt. On one hand, you are trying to trust the Lord and believe that He is coming through, yet in your mind, the clock is ticking. Sometimes you just want to go back to the Lord and say, "Hey, Lord, remember me? I'm your boy! I'm still here. Whassup with the delay? Hey, don't forget what I asked you—don't forget my prayer." (I know you probably never pray to the Lord like that, but trust me, I know how the sisters felt!)

Then things got worse: Lazarus died. They had the funeral. They buried him in a tomb. Still no word from Jesus. No voice of God. Nothing.

Then we come to John 11:17, where it says that by the time Jesus got there, Lazarus had been dead and in the tomb for four days. I mean, the brother *stank*—let's be real; dead four days. Verse 20 says that when Martha heard that He was coming, she went out to meet Him. Sentences like that in Scripture don't give the full ethos, the complete description of the range of emotions that must have been running rampant in that little town when Jesus came down Main Street, Bethany. Words simply cannot possibly convey the tenseness, the rush of conflicting emotions, the anger, curiosity, pain, disillusionment, the utter, sheer confusion that had to be coursing through the people as they watched Him turn the corner and tread toward the Lazarus house, probably in a very comfortable, measured, unhurried pace, followed by His ever-present entourage of followers.

You see the words on the page, but you sense that Martha probably did a little more than just "went to meet Him" as the verse describes. She may have started out walking, then broke into a trot and then began running pell-mell at Him, bursting with emotions—resentment, hurt, puzzlement, who knows. Martha might have cried out, "Here He comes!" Their excitement at seeing Him may have been tempered with disillusionment at the late arrival of the Lord (not realizing that God is *never* late), along with deep sorrow at the loss of their brother and maybe even not a small feeling of anger.

In verse 21, Martha said to Jesus, "Lord, if You had been here, my brother would not have died." That's one way to interpret what happened. On the other hand, it might not be a stretch to imagine Martha might have also said something like, "Uh-huh. Here He comes. Oh, *now* You come. Where You been, Jesus? You didn't get our message?" I wonder if she had an attitude going. "If you'd a been here, he wouldn'ta died! Four days on! What were You *doing?*—You were only an hour's walk away. Now the man's dead! He *loved* You!"

I highly recommend that you read Oswald Chambers's classic and timeless daily devotional, *My Utmost for His Highest.* The magnificently inspiring collection of daily readings was first published in 1935, but the truths and revelations that come through Dr. Chambers continues to change lives decades later. I believe Dr. Chambers would have directed Mary and Martha to read his devotional for July 30. He would tell them they need to learn what he calls "the discipline of disillusionment." Martha said, "If you had been here, my brother would not have died." There is much revelation in the phrase, "If you had been here." If you get nothing else out of this book, please get this:

What you believe about God will determine how you live your life.
Martha assumed that wherever Jesus was, bad things would
never happen. She believed that the negative realities and possibilities of her life would not occur when Jesus was around. *If
You had been here, none of this would have happened.* What Martha
had not learned was the discipline of disillusionment.

The word "disillusion" means to "negate the illusion." It
means that there is a false impression that must be contradicted. However, that which must be contradicted was an illusion in the first place. Oswald Chambers says that the illusion
(the picture that you have of a truth that frames your reality of
that truth) will determine what you expect from that truth. In
other words, we paint a picture of what we think things ought
to look like. Then, once we get that picture in our mind, expectations grow out of our concept of that truth. That is, we expect certain things to happen based on what we believe the
truth is. For example, newlyweds have an image of what marriage ought to be like. Their fulfillment within that marriage
is, to a great degree, dependent upon the image and expectations each person had of their mate by the time they said "I do"
at the altar. The degree to which those expectations are not met
will leave them disillusioned. The question is: *Is their concept of
marriage reality, or is their concept of marriage an illusion?* If what
they believe is an illusion, then when the truth is revealed, the
illusion will be shattered.

Martha had an illusion, an image, of what life in Christ
ought to be. She believed that as long as Jesus was in the house,
people wouldn't die, wouldn't get sick, bad things wouldn't
happen, there would be no negativity, no storms, no trials, no
problems. Everything would be hunky-dory because Jesus was
in the house. That was her image of Him. But is that image
of Him reality or is it an illusion? Martha's expectations were
birthed from the image she had of her relationship with the

Lord and who she thought He was up until the time her brother Lazarus died. If Jesus did not fulfill her image and expectations, her illusion would be destroyed and she would live in disillusionment and letdown. Her expectation was that if He had been here, Lazarus's death would not have happened. Her disillusionment led to her frustration and disappointment because Jesus didn't act like the Jesus she thought she knew.

But the Jesus she thought she knew was about to take her understanding of Him to a whole new level.

God Doesn't Ask, "How High?"
When We Tell Him to Jump

What do you do when God doesn't act like God? When you have a concept of what you think He should do and how He ought to operate, what happens when He does not fit your image? Your image of Him might well be an illusion; and your disappointment would grow out of the disillusionment of the contradiction of what you expected of Him and who He actually is.

This point can be illustrated by marriage: If I have an idea of what a wife or a husband should do and should not do, then I have a concept of what marriage is supposed to look like and how spouses are supposed to behave and treat one another. However, the degree to which the realities of life enter in and create a distortion of that image, my life then moves into a place of discouragement based on my disillusionment. This is because people in this culture and generation, for the most part, do not get their images from revelations of life; they get them from TV, Internet, movies, books, soap operas, blogs, Facebook, friends' points of view, parents, from practically everyplace *except* where the true revelations of this life occur: from *relationship with God*. This is because (as I stated in chapter 1) people in this culture and generation tend to want neither revelation from

God nor true relationship with Him. They only want information. However, information only changes our thoughts—the way we *think* about an issue. The more information and input we have about something, the more we might think differently about it, but information alone will not change our *behavior* about it. Only *belief* about something can change our behavior concerning that something; and the only thing that alters, creates or affects belief is *revelation*. Concerning the things of God, revelation comes to us through the Holy Spirit. Once our belief has been altered by revelation, then our behavior will change.

Our image and belief about God determine how we live and how we behave. Therefore, our image and our expectation of God must be based on His revelation to us about Himself, and not on our image of Him—unless our image of Him was produced by His revelation of Himself. I know that sounds like doubletalk, but our lives are shaped and transformed only by the application of the true revelation of God and our relationship with Him. Putting this in the context of the story of Lazarus, if I was Mary's friend, when she called me I would have hightailed it right on down the road to Bethany because she and Martha and Lazarus were my close friends and that is my idea about how good friends should, in our humanness, treat each other. But when Jesus showed up four days later, if I were the sisters, I would have struggled with disillusionment because He would not have been acting the way *I* expected Him to act. He was "supposed" to come quickly, step into that room and heal my brother immediately.

God was supposed to come and step in before I lost my house.
He was supposed to come and step in before my marriage crumbled.
Before my child died.
Before my momma left me.
Before I went bankrupt.
Before I lost my job.

What kind of God is this who cannot show up when you call Him? I thought when you call Him, He hears you and He answers? Have you ever been in a situation with God where He didn't do what you expected of Him, didn't show up when you wanted Him to show up, didn't answer the way you wanted Him to? What do you do when you hear the sound of silence and God isn't acting like God? When He doesn't ask "How high?" when you tell Him to jump?

Psalms of Lament

The sound of silence forces us to look at ourselves and forces us to look at God again. There is a category of more than 50 psalms called Psalms of Lament. These psalms are individual or corporate pleas and prayers to a God who is not doing what is expected of Him. These psalms are spoken from discouragement, prayed or sung with brokenness of heart, sometimes in anger or outrage. Occasionally, they are expressed with bitterness or with metaphorical (or literal) shaking of the fist at God. Often they are sung in desperation: "Dear God, where are You? Why are You letting this happen to me?" They depict the desperations of life, when the desperate call out to a divine God in desperate situations. They are speaking from within a storm or from a pit and cannot hear God.

I've always wondered why there would be more than 50 psalms of lament. Why would God put these in the Bible? One-third of the psalms are psalms of lament, where people are going through things that make no sense to them. They don't understand their circumstances. There's no logic to it. Oh, they know they may have messed up, but they oftentimes say, "Lord, I didn't mess up *that* bad." Have you ever prayed that prayer? "Come on, Lord, can't You cut me some slack?"

One morning I was listening to my friend Steve Harvey on "The Steve Harvey Morning Show." Time and time again, Steve's opening remarks that start his show have blessed and encouraged me. This particular morning, Steve was talking about prayer. He often says, "Don't be too proud to pray." I smiled and laughed out loud as he talked about how he prays. I laughed because it sounded so much like me and the way I pray. Steve said something like this: "Sometimes I just go to God and say, 'Can You cut Your boy some slack? Can You give me a break?'" I can't tell you how many times I pray like that. I really don't think we need to come to God with a lot of fancy religious talk. I think we can just come to Him and be real. We can talk from the heart. And sometimes, like Steve Harvey, my best prayer is, "Lord, can You cut Your boy some slack?!"

Without knowing it, many of us have spoken some of the ideas in the psalms of lament. Actually, I think sooner or later it happens to every one of us. One of the most popular ones of all goes like this: "My God, My God, why have You forsaken Me?" (Ps. 22:1)—*whoa!*—wait a minute . . . that sounds just like the same prayer Jesus lamented while He was hanging on a cross between two thieves. You mean Jesus, the Son of the living God, called upon His father and couldn't get an answer? That's right. Even the Son of the living God—the Only Begotten of the Father—who hung on a cross, and all He (even *HE*) heard from heaven was . . . silence. Jesus knew the Scriptures, which means He knew the verse that said, "I will not leave you nor forsake you" (Josh. 1:5). He is the same Jesus who, in His divinity, said, "I will never leave you." And yet He, in His humanity, is the same Jesus who also said, "Why have you left me?" (see Mark 15:34). Over 50 psalms of lament, and even Jesus had to suffer the sound of silence.

Isn't it interesting that we get upset when we can't hear from God? Yet, do you ever wonder how God feels when He can't hear from *you*? We get upset when we feel we have to wait on God. We'll wait on love. We'll wait on a husband. We'll wait on a job. We'll wait in line to go to the movies. Yet, we put God on the clock, and we get upset when we don't hear from Him. When we expect that level of attention or service from Him in our time of need and He doesn't deliver, we are essentially lamenting that He isn't behaving like one of us. Yet, God is not a man (see Num. 23:19; 1 Sam. 15:29); He is the one who "forms the mountains, creates the wind, and reveals his thoughts to man, he who turns dawn to darkness, and treads the high places of the earth" (Amos 4:13, *NIV*).

If Mary didn't hear from God, and Martha didn't hear from God, and Lazarus didn't hear from God, and Jesus Himself didn't hear from God, then there are pretty good odds that, since the normalcy of your walk with Christ is an ebb and flow of hearing and waiting, there will be times when you are walking with Him but you cannot hear Him. If Jesus the Christ went through it, and you're supposed to be following Him and being conformed to His image, then trust me, my friend, your day is coming when you expect to hear a word from Him and instead you will hear . . . *nothing*. It doesn't mean He is gone. He *always is*; He's the great I AM. He is merely building you, stretching you, growing you.

Search Me, Lord!

So what do we do in the meantime? When you are waiting to hear God's voice and nothing happens, have you ever thought about taking a little inventory? One of the first things we should do is examine ourselves: ask the question, "Why me?" For four days Mary and Martha waited for Jesus. I guarantee you, one of them said to the other something like, "Girl, c'mere. Do you think the last time He was here maybe we offended Him? Did you serve Him some bad food? Did you burn His bagel?"

There is a conversation we go through, often with ourselves, when we hear nothing from God. Maybe we did something wrong. Maybe it's our fault. Maybe He's not coming because we did something bad, and He's holding it against us. After a while, when things are still off the track, we kind of take an inventory. "Well, now . . . let's see here, Lord. Uh, last Friday night, You know, I didn't repent of that thing I did—and I'm sorry about that, Lord. And then I missed church two Sundays ago because I was up late Saturday night, going to that thing I really shouldn't have gone to." We go through a whole list because we want to clean the slate and make sure that whatever the holdup is, we at least are standing repentant and forgiven. Self-examination is a great place to start.

Eliminate the Sin Issue

The next thing to do while waiting on a word from God is to eliminate the sin issue. Isaiah 59:2 says, "Your iniquities have separated you from your God; your sins have hidden his face from you, so that he will not hear" (NIV). Ask God to show you if there is anything in your life that's hindering the revelation of His will. Rather than pray, "Lord, hear my prayer," pray a prayer that He will truly hear, something like this: "Lord, show me my sin." He'll answer that one. Pray something like: "Search me, O God, and know my heart; try me, and know my anxieties; and see if there is any wicked way in me, and lead me in the way everlasting (Ps. 139:23-24). And if You find anything that shouldn't be, take it out and straighten me out, Lord. I want to be right with You. I want to be whole."

Eliminate the sin issue.

Thomas Dorsey, a pioneer and, to some, the father of African American gospel music, penned a song that is both a prayer to the Lord and a product of a mind that wants to elim-

inate the sin issue. Gospel greats Mahalia Jackson, Donnie Mc-
Clurken and Rickey Dillard sampled, revised and made variations
on this beautiful Dorsey theme:

> *Search me Lord, search me Lord*
> *Turn the light from heaven on my soul*
> *If you find anything that shouldn't be*
> *Take it out and straighten me.*
>
> REVEREND THOMAS A. DORSEY, "SEARCH ME LORD"

God Is Never in a Hurry

After you've examined yourself and eliminated sin, the next step
is to revise your image of God. God, who was and who is and who
is to come, is never in a hurry. He can't be late because He is the
God who says, "I AM." That means that He always is. And if He
always is, He can never be *was*. If He always is, He can never be late
because by the time *late* rolls around, He already *is*. Understand
that God is *never* late. Your clock may be wrong, but God is always on time.

When we say "late," we are making a judgment based on time.
But God is the Ancient of Days, He is the Alpha and Omega, the Beginning and the End. He is from *A* to *Z* and everything in between.
Time does not age Him, and ages cannot time Him. He is always on
time. My mother and the old saints were right when they said, "He
may not come when you call Him, but He's always on time!"

Remember His Image of You

The fourth thing to do is to remember what God thinks about
you. John 11:4-15 tells us what Jesus was thinking when He received word that Lazarus was gravely ill. What should you do
while you're waiting to hear His voice? Here's a good strategy for

survival: *Remember His image of you!* We struggle with the inconsistency of our image of Him, but He has an image of each of us, one that is unchangeable. Jeremiah 29:4-16 tells us what Jesus was thinking in John 11 as He was making His way from Jerusalem to Bethany, four days after Lazarus was laid in the tomb: "I know the thoughts that I think toward you, says the LORD, thoughts of peace and not of evil, to give you a future and a hope" (Jer. 29:11).

God *never* lets His faithful children down. NEVER. He's thinking about you even when you can't hear Him. His thoughts of you are not thoughts of evil; they are thoughts of peace. He speaks peace into your life—peace while you're waiting, peace while you're discouraged, peace while you're disillusioned, peace while you're frustrated. He speaks peace and hope until your circumstances change.

Back to Mary, Martha and Lazarus: At last, in John 11:17, here comes Jesus, walking casually toward Bethany, four days late, long after Lazarus has died and been buried in a tomb. Mary and Martha have been waiting and waiting. Here He finally comes. The whole city is involved now. Mary and Martha are probably feeling a measure of public embarrassment because Jesus hadn't shown up "in time," and everybody thought He was such a close friend of their family.

Mary and Martha did not know what Jesus was thinking as they were stuck there, waiting on Him. They only knew Jesus was too late. Yet, Jesus gets there, and what does He do? He raises Lazarus from the dead. And He gently reminds them, "Did I not tell you that if you believed, you would see the glory of God?" (John 11:40, *NIV*).

What, then, is this business of knowing the voice of God all about? It's about *trust*. Once you learn His voice, trust His word. Remember, His timing is not our timing; our timing is human, but His timing is *perfect*.

To Truly Hear Him Is to Fully Heed Him

It cannot be repeated too often: The ability to discern God's voice in our spirit comes only from *relationship* with Him. Relationship with God assumes dialog and conversation. No healthy relationship consists of just one person doing all of the talking all of the time. God wants us to have an *ongoing* conversation *with* Him throughout our lives. Whether it is for clarification, education or revelation, God has things to tell us that are important and applicable to building productive, wholesome, fulfilling lives that honor Him and help and encourage others.

The first step in developing relationship with God is simply to *listen to Him*. The more we train ourselves to listen to God, the more we are able to know His unique voice in our spirit. Hearing and knowing His voice then open the pathway for Him to reveal more of Himself, His plans and His ways to us, just as He did with young Samuel. Revelation from God is what builds our trust in God. For His revelation is always designed to give us direction, to build us up, to further His plans for His beloved children and to glorify Himself.

I want to leave you with the words of a song you probably have never heard of. It was on a recording that may have sold a few hundred copies—at most. Dr. Margaret Douroux wrote it, and I was the organist on it. Its message is inspiring and encouraging, challenging and comforting.

The Lord is speaking – to you; to you.
The Lord is speaking to you
Can't you hear what He's saying?
Why are you waiting?
The Lord—is speaking to you.
He speaks through an earthquake,
And through a storm tossed sea.
He speaks through a silent night

So sweet and quietly.
Can't you hear what He's saying?
Why are you waiting?
The Lord is speaking—to you.

DR. MARGARET DOUROUX, "THE LORD IS SPEAKING TO YOU"[1]

It is my prayer that this examination of how to hear the voice of God in our increasingly noisy and tumultuous world has helped you to learn to know His voice whenever He speaks to you. Once you have learned His voice, I encourage you to simply *do* as He says . . . and watch your life blossom.

Note
1. Dr. Margaret Douroux, "The Lord Is Speaking to You," © Earl Pleasant Publishing. Used by permission.

About the Author

For more than 25 years, Kenneth C. Ulmer, Ph.D., has been Senior Pastor of Faithful Central Bible Church in Los Angeles. He is also past president of The King's University in Los Angeles (where he is a founding board member, an adjunct Professor of Preaching and Leadership, and serves as the Dean of The King's Oxford University Summer Program, England). In 2000 Dr. Ulmer's church acquired The Great Western Forum (previous home of the Lakers professional basketball team), which the ministry operated as a commercial entertainment venue.

Dr. Ulmer participated in the study of Ecumenical Liturgy and Worship at Magdalene College at Oxford University in England, has served as an instructor in Pastoral Ministry and Homiletics at Grace Theological Seminary, as an instructor of African American Preaching at Fuller Theological Seminary, as an adjunct professor at Biola University (where he served on the Board of Trustees) and as an adjunct professor at Pepperdine University. He also served as a mentor in the Doctor of Ministry degree program at United Theological Seminary, in Ohio.

He received his Bachelor of Arts degree in Broadcasting and Music from the University of Illinois. After accepting his call to the ministry, Dr. Ulmer was ordained at Mount Moriah Missionary Baptist Church in Los Angeles, and shortly afterward founded Macedonia Bible Baptist Church in San Pedro, California. He has studied at Pepperdine University, Hebrew Union College, the University of Judaism and Christ Church and Magdalene College at Oxford University in England. He earned a Ph.D. from Grace Graduate School of Theology, in Long Beach, California (west coast Campus of Grace Theological Seminary), and his Doctor of Ministry from United Theological Seminary.

He was awarded an Honorary Doctor of Divinity degree from Southern California School of Ministry.

Pastor Ulmer was consecrated as Bishop of Christian Education of the Full Gospel Baptist Church Fellowship, where he served on the Bishops' Council. He has served on the Board of Directors of The Gospel Music Workshop of America, the Pastor's Advisory Council to the mayor of the City of Inglewood, California, and on the Board of Trustees of Southern California School of Ministry. He is currently Presiding Bishop over Macedonia International Bible Fellowship, based in Johannesburg, South Africa, which is an association of pastors representing ministries in South Africa, Jerusalem and the U.S.

Dr. Ulmer is a recipient of The King's College Apostelos Christou Award, which is annually presented to leaders who characterize the passion and values of the Christian faith through leadership that has notably penetrated the contemporary culture.

He is served in literary, editorial, film and television endeavors by Los Angeles author and writer M. Rutledge McCall.

Also by Kenneth Ulmer

Kenneth Ulmer is the Associate Editor of *The New Spirit Filled Life Bible* (Thomas Nelson Publishers), and has written several books, including *Making Your Money Count: Why We Have It & How to Manage It*; *A New Thing* (a reflection on the Full Gospel Baptist Movement); *Spiritually Fit to Run the Race* (a guide to godly living); *In His Image: An Intimate Reflection of God* (an update of his book *The Anatomy of God*); *The Champion in You* (about developing champions for God's Kingdom on earth); and *The Power of Money: How to Avoid a Devil's Snare*.

What Is True Biblical Prosperity?

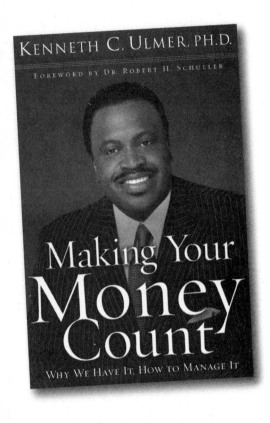

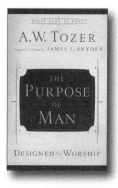
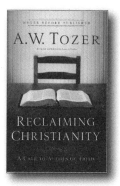
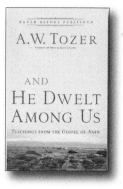
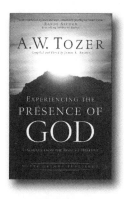
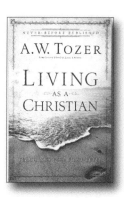
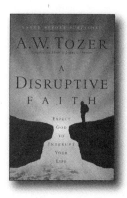

202 493 3471